Spheres of Insurrection

Critical South

*The publication of this series is supported by the
International Consortium of Critical Theory Programs
funded by the Andrew W. Mellon Foundation.*

Series editors: Natalia Brizuela, Victoria Collis-Buthelezi and
Leticia Sabsay

Leonor Arfuch, *Memory and Autobiography*
Paula Biglieri and Luciana Cadahia, *Seven Essays on Populism*
Aimé Césaire, *Resolutely Black*
Bolívar Echeverría, *Modernity and "Whiteness"*
Diego Falconí Trávez, *From Ashes to Text*
Celso Furtado, *The Myth of Economic Development*
Eduardo Grüner, *The Haitian Revolution*
Ailton Krenak, *Life is Not Useful*
Premesh Lalu, *Undoing Apartheid*
Karima Lazali, *Colonial Trauma*
María Pia López, *Not One Less*
Achille Mbembe and Felwine Sarr, *The Politics of Time*
Achille Mbembe and Felwine Sarr, *To Write the Africa World*
Valentin-Yves Mudimbe, *The Scent of the Father*
Pablo Oyarzun, *Doing Justice*
Néstor Perlongher, *Plebeian Prose*
Bento Prado Jr., *Error, Illusion, Madness*
Nelly Richard, *Eruptions of Memory*
Suely Rolnik, *Spheres of Insurrection*
Silvia Rivera Cusicanqui, *Ch'ixinakax utxiwa*
Tendayi Sithole, *The Black Register*
Maboula Soumahoro, *Black is the Journey, Africana the Name*
Dénètem Touam Bona, *Fugitive, Where Are You Running?*

Spheres of Insurrection
Notes on Decolonizing the Unconscious

Suely Rolnik

Translated by Sergio Delgado Moya

polity

Originally published in Portuguese as *Esferas da insurreção. Notas para uma vida não cafetinada* in 2018 by n-1 edições. Copyright © Suely Rolnik, 2018. All rights reserved.

This English translation © Polity Press, 2023

Excerpts from *What is Philosophy?* by Gilles Deleuze and Felix Guattari, Verso, 1994, included by permission of the publishers. Reproduced with permission of the Licensor through PLSclear.

Polity Press
65 Bridge Street
Cambridge CB2 1UR, UK

Polity Press
111 River Street
Hoboken, NJ 07030, USA

All rights reserved. Except for the quotation of short passages for the purpose of criticism and review, no part of this publication may be reproduced, stored in a retrieval system or transmitted, in any form or by any means, electronic, mechanical, photocopying, recording or otherwise, without the prior permission of the publisher.

ISBN-13: 978-1-5095-5285-6- hardback
ISBN-13: 978-1-5095-5286-3 – paperback

A catalogue record for this book is available from the British Library.

Library of Congress Control Number: 2022949183

Typeset in 10.5 on 12pt Sabon
by Fakenham Prepress Solutions, Fakenham, Norfolk NR21 8NL
Printed and bound in Great Britain by TJ Books Ltd, Padstow, Cornwall

The publisher has used its best endeavours to ensure that the URLs for external websites referred to in this book are correct and active at the time of going to press. However, the publisher has no responsibility for the websites and can make no guarantee that a site will remain live or that the content is or will remain appropriate.

Every effort has been made to trace all copyright holders, but if any have been overlooked the publisher will be pleased to include any necessary credits in any subsequent reprint or edition.

For further information on Polity, visit our website:
politybooks.com

To Eugenia, inaugural lucidity

It is always a question of freeing life wherever it is imprisoned, or of tempting it into an uncertain combat.

Gilles Deleuze and Félix Guattari, *What Is Philosophy?* (New York: Columbia University Press, 1994): 171.

Contents

Introduction – Stefano Harney	ix
Prelude: Words Blooming Out of the Lumps in Our Throats	xix
Colonial-Capitalistic Unconscious	1
Macro- and Micropolitical Insurgency: Links and Dissimilarities	59
The New Modality of Coup: A Series in Three Seasons	95
Finale: Ten Suggestions for the Practice of Decolonizing the Unconscious	150
Notes	153

Introduction
Suely Rolnick's Untimely Insurgency
Stefano Harney

When he was in prison on charges that were later to be thrown out, then former President Luis Inácio Lula da Silva gave an interview to the investigative journalist Glenn Greenwald. Greenwald asks what could be interpreted as a question critical of Lula and his time in government. He asks why, given how well big business fared under his administration, capitalists both big and small in Brazil seemed to despise him so much. Lula does not appear to take the question as a criticism, or rather perhaps he does not react to it because he has come to realize the criticism is somehow beside the point. In any case, Lula gives what Suely Rolnick might call, in the vital essays that follow, a micropolitical answer. Lula says that the only way he can explain this hostility is by way of the changes in Brazilian society that took place during his eight years in office (and during President Dilma Rousseff's truncated continuation of Worker's Party rule after him). Through the introduction of family support, affirmative action, employment law, and a host of other measures, Lula and his party greatly enlarged the number of people who participated in Brazil's official economy. And Lula says of those who nonetheless hate him, that they hate him simply because of who now stands next to them in the line at the cinema, the airport and the supermarket. Lula, the embodiment of a macropolitical energy, then as now, perhaps reflecting in his imposed otium, gives us a micropolitical response.

x Introduction

What Lula is able to see is how these changes, attributed to him, activated into vicious reaction the settler colonial desire for the slave and servant society that as Suely Rolnick will tell us, Brazil in large part remains. She writes that the viciousness toward Lula and the rise of now-former President Jair Bolsonaro 'really reveals ... that the visceral presence of the colonial and slave-holding tradition in Brazil never ceased to exist in the subjectivity of its middle and elite classes.' This presence is somehow out-of-history as Brazil concludes its 200th year anniversary as a republic. The time of Brazil that accompanies this crucial publication – making Suely Rolnick's seminal essays available to English-speaking readers – is a time of relief. It is a time of the return to power of President Lula, after five years of environmental, social, and economic nihilistic mismanagement under the far-right former President Jair Bolsonaro. For Lula himself it is a time marked by his path from jail to the presidency. It is a return. But this time is also full with what is out of this time. Returns that never seem to stop. The last five years have brought memories and fears of the 1964-1985 military dictatorship to the surface where they linger still, peddling the reactive desires of Ordem e Progresso, the motto of the Brazilian republic. The phrase itself is cut out from the time of the French sociologist August Comte who said 'love as a principle, the order as a foundation, progress as a goal.' In the last five years love seemed to have returned from its excising, but as love for the leader, life-killing love. More untimely still was the nearly half of the population who voted to continue the ghoulish settler colonial performance as Brazil under Bolsonaro renewed its desire to 'open' its interior and build its national destiny, by the violent imposition of property, labour, and profit in the Amazon. Suely Rolnick concludes of the swing of support behind Bolsonaro that 'what the elites behind these operations did not consider was that the high degree of morbidity in the subjectivity of Bolsonaro (a morbidity easily detectable in his personal and political history) would lead him to become the leader of a fascist form of populism.' But perhaps they should have known better.

***

Another way to look at this renewed settler desire is to ask what kind of decolonizing is called for in Brazil today? The answer is

Introduction *xi*

that the kind of decolonizing Brazil requires is the anti-colonial kind. As in the United States, we must say that the anti-colonial movement has yet to succeed in Brazil. This is true at the level of desire as much as at the level of property and profit. Anti-colonialism remains the demand of the day. Decolonizing these societies is therefore always an untimely project. And this is precisely why we need Suely Rolnick's work now more than ever, even if now is ever. Because as Lula's answer reveals the struggle to decolonize the colony that Brazil remains, that the US remains, that Israel remains, that Australia remains, that Chile remains and so on, this struggle must take place at the molecular level and not just the molar level. The one continues because the other continues, but the other continues because the one continues. Thus, so too, the two struggles continue.

But in making this statement about micropolitical and macropolitical struggles confronting us, two problems immediately arise, problems with which Suely Rolnick will help us. The first of these problems is that these two forms of struggle do not work in harmony. They do not mirror each other. They do not facilitate a common topography. The insubordination of micropolitics, as Suely Rolnick calls it, provokes not just settler colonial rule, but also something in macropolitical struggle. The macropolitical struggle, the forces of the Left, react to the micropolitical announcements with a strategy of containment. Thus, the first problem we are confronted with is a problem for the Left. The reason for this is that the macropolitical struggle in most historical instances chooses a pragmatic path. The Left often does so sincerely. It often achieves gains by doing so. But what it does not reckon with is that what has been presented as the pragmatic path is in fact a road to absolutism. Because pragmatism is an absolutist ideology. I do not mean this in the anti-communist way such charges are often levelled. In fact, it is not even a charge. It is simply to say that in order for the macropolitical Left to fight at the level of rights, democracy, and sovereignty, as it often must, it is necessary for it to take on the language and the logic of the one. Or as Suely Rolnick calls it, the logic of identitarian politics. Far from being reasonable or moderate, when the Left takes a pragmatic position, it opens micropolitical struggles to great danger.

Because pragmatism of this kind always reinstalls the language and logic of the one, the individual, as the foundation for

Introduction

politics. This reduction to the one individual, and the many individuals, forecloses the collective enunciations of desire. It spurs the very individuation upon which settler colonialism thrives. The subject, the citizen, the voter, the party, the nation, one nation indivisible, as the American like to say. This is the one who may stand before the law, who may represent others, who may make policy, and who may own property. This is the one who is sovereign, powered by the delusion of self-sufficiency, self-authorship, and self-development. This is the one who holds and enacts this delusion and appoints himself to diagnose the incompleteness of the others not by denying their individuality but by forcing upon them only enough oneness to bring them into the world, the rapacious world of property, finance, labour, and sexual demand. This is the one who says he's the one. And although the exception is going on all around him, he can only see it in his own violation. As Cedric Robinson argues in his classic *Terms of Order*, all Western macropolitics from Right to Left is based on the completeness of the one as the unit of politics. And a pragmatic politics demands completeness.

It is this complete one that allows us to make what at first may seem to be a needlessly provocative statement: that representative democracy, one man-one vote democracy is not the opposite of settler colonialism but a tool of its imposition and rule. Indeed, politics in its reductive, reactive emplotment of the one *is* at base a tool of white supremacism. It is hard for the Left to admit these metaphysical foundations of politics. Though white people seem to know this perfectly well. Because whenever democracy does not result in white supremacist rule, as in the exceptional years of PT government then and now, it is deemed not be democracy but to be instead a stolen election. The history of US coup-mongering against elected governments in the wider region, including the tacit support of President Barack Obama and Secretary Hilary Clinton's for the 'slow motion' coup against Dilma Rousseff, should be enough to state the point. (Then Vice President Joe Biden was the point man on that one by the way.) And here again is indispensability of Suely Rolnick's thought. The pragmatism of the Left – heightened in moments of self-defense against 'the coup' – leads it to ask, and then soon to demand, the same of its micropolitical surrounds, and this must be resisted. This pragmatic demand, which uses the love we retain for those who ask, uses them against our mutual love, to hide its

Introduction *xiii*

ultimately absolutist white supremacy. This corrosive demand comes in a number of forms: a call for unity, an exhortation to scale-up, a plea to be strategic, or a return to 'class analysis.' But in order for us to answer this demand, micropolitics must give up its insurgent project of total disorder and identify itself, identify with itself, realize itself and become one completely. As Rolnick writes 'the dominant cartographies' of politics 'seek to prevent the insubordination of the micropolitical.' Throughout these essays Suely Rolnick grapples with this problematic articulation of the macropolitical and the micropolitical and its consequences for the revolt of the unconsciousnesses.

But in Brazil, as in other settler colonial societies, or what Suely Rolnick names pimp-colonial-capitalist societies, the articulation between the micropolitical and the macropolitical is not just fraught on the Left, but also confronts us on and in the Right. This is the second problem, especially since daily life for all of us, or almost all of us, takes place on the Right. By this I mean our habits are mediated by capitalist markets, media, and social institutions that are persistently aligned with the Right and infused with its purpose. We shop, we browse, we work, we text, and we play in this space, regardless of the macropolitical moment. Suely Rolnick suggests this is why we (are forced to) produce so many 'novelties' rather than new ways of living, new potentialities. Brazilians will still be living daily life on the Right under the new Lula administration. Americans are living daily life on the Right under Joe Biden. Of course, many of us also live daily life against the Right. And this means rebelling not just against the overt compulsions of the Right. It also means there is an ongoing insurgency against the reactive desire of the Right, especially as it manifest in such settler societies.

I was reminded of the entanglement of the macropolitical and the micropolitical one day recently in conversation in Rio with my friend Denise Ferreira da Silva, the brilliant philosopher and artist. I said something about the way the Right was stoking fear of communism despite the fact Lula had proved himself moderate in his previous terms. I was surprised, I told her, that this was effective. Denise replied that in Brazil when you say communist, you say black. It was a micropolitical lesson for me. Not clear until it was said, and so clear once it was said. Anti-black desire in Brazil, which is perhaps a more accurate way to put it than anti-blackness, wells up from the settler colonial unconscious *xiv*   Introduction

like a toxic effluviant. And it mixes with the overtly macropolitical energies of the Right to the extent that the two feed each other and are hard to separate. When we fight in the realm of the macropolitical in settler colonial societies in those necessary moments of collective self-defense, we are also always fighting on the terrain of desire, reactive desire. Rhetoric emanating from the Right about finance, or education, or health, or even foreign policy is all the time fused to mobilization of reactive desires for dominance over the other, but most especially to anti-black desire. Living as we do involuntarily on the Right, many of us are invited into this mobilization. It is the brilliance of these essays that Suely Rolnick shows us how to resist and to announce our own desires instead, inspired by the ongoing insurgency against settler colonialism carried on by indigenous communities, favela organizers, quilombo communities, feminist organizations, queer communities, and dissident and resistant artists, workers, and others. President Lula's victory provides a measure of self-defense for these always out-of-time insurgencies.

* * *

Despite this moment of untimely relief, Suely Rolnick reminds us that the coup is not a thing of the past. In odorous mouth of Jair Bolsonaro, in the slow-motion coup against Dilma Rouseff, in Honduras coup of 2009 or in Bolivia in 2019, the coup returns as a weapon of white supremacist democracy. But it has increasingly been augmented by another weapon on the Right that also draws from the common commitment to the figure of the complete one, in this case the individual who can stand before the law. Because the rights-bearing subject is also the kind of figure that can have rights taken away as part of the fiction that such rights resided inside the one in the first place. Lawfare has always been deployed against the poor, against indigenous and quilombo communities, and against the poor, workers, women, and queer people, even if these rights-bearing near subjects were adjudged incapable of bearing the rights. But in the last decades it has increasingly become a weapon against the macropolitical Left.

At the time of his interview with Lula, Glenn Greenwald was one of the motive forces behind *The Intercept* investigative news platform, including its specific Brazilian edition. It was *The Intercept* that would publish evidence, in form of leaked

Introduction xv

telephone records including voice and text messages, of a conspiracy between the judge in Lula's case, Sergio Moro, and the prosecutors of the case. Moro was heard effectively coaching the prosecutors, while the prosecutors were heard admitting that the case was being pursued for political not criminal reasons, a fact with which they were evidently quite pleased. But Moro was not just any judge, rather he was the key judge in the massive 'Lava Jato' corruption investigations encompassing business leaders, politicians of many parties, and major firms, and extending beyond Brazil as far as Peru and Mexico. Suely Rolnick tracks these investigations at the level of their macropolitical lawfare, and at the level of their micropolitical drama in the third and final of her essays comprising this book. If Moro was dirty (and he was), dozens of high-profile convictions of businessmen and politicians might be overturned. The charges against Lula were quietly dropped with the acquiescence of Brazil's Supreme Court. And again what Suely Rolnick teaches us about this drama is precisely that it played out as manufactured desire on television screens in Brazil at the same time that it played out in the courts. The micropolitical reactive desires produced by the drama fed and were fed by the ideology of the law, of rights, and of the carceral state as safe-guarding those rights by denying them. Sergio Moro is now an elected senator.

* * *

In the face of this constant return of settler violence, Suely Rolnick urges us not to succumb to what Fred Moten and I have called the 'subject reaction' in which we mistake the contingent efforts at self-defence as essential properties of life. There are constant threats to bodies and rights under settler violence, but this should not convince us we have bodies or rights even as we defend them. Suely Rolnick asks us to pay attention to what else is going on even under extreme duress – the experiments and exercises in the extrasensorial, extracognitive, and the extrasentimenal as she puts it. In place of the interpersonal, of interpersonal relations, instating the hazardous figure of the person, an extraentanglement must be militantly preserved and practiced. 'Micropolitics tends to announce through resonances the potentialization of life,' she writes, and it is to the rehearsal and revision of these resonances we must turn.

xvi   Introduction

One way to think of this is through the decolonization of the *other* senses. The decolonization of the hierarchy and weaponization of the five senses must continue. But especially through the work being done around neurodiversity by scholars like Erin Manning, we are aware that the other senses have also felt the violent imposition of settlement. Proprioceptive, vestibular, interoceptive senses are the senses of movement, balance, and the 'internal' which colonialization assigned to the individuated body, but which also exist in the extraentanglement. Colonization has deployed several strategies against these other senses. The first strategy of colonialization is to suppress these senses as senses, exile them from the others and from serious cultivation under colonialism. Hence the prominence of only the five senses. Another strategy is to reduce these other senses to instincts, to group them with the animalistic. And if they must be acknowledged they are put to the specific uses of colonialism. The vestibular is valued only for its uprightness and control, for the balletic. It reinforces the driven stake of the settler and his flag. The interoceptive becomes the symptomatic, which science will address and clarify while substituting its own professional knowledge and expertise. The proprioceptive shows up even more of as a symptom, despite being the only one that admits of anything carrying the extraindividual. The sense of movement in the hands of the social sciences becomes the madness of crowds, the dangerous irrationality of the masses, of collective movement. And any deviation from the colonial use of these other senses is quickly pathologized.

But decolonizing these senses may have much to offer us as part of our accumulation of other desires urged on by these essays. The sense of movement that is named by proprioception may appear the most obvious for a decolonial recovery of common movement. But a simple reversal might well leave us with the classic macropolitical model on the Left of a worker's movement or a civil rights movement. But let us look for a second at the micropolitical movement of the civil rights movement in the United States as an example of a different decolonialization, or perhaps again an anti-colonial decolonization. Oral histories of that movement challenge the dominant narrative in two important ways. First, as great historian Robin D.G. Kelley points out, these struggles were local struggles. Their macropolitical unity unravels as a highly differentiated set of localized

Introduction   *xvii*

political becomings. Second, the dominant narrative of desire, the desire for integration, is also questioned by a people's history of these movements. Again and again for instance, parents of children who were 'integrated' into white schools insisted in oral testimonies they did not want their children to integrate with white children. What they did want were the resources to be found where white children were schooled. These micropolitical resistances in movement are the qualities of movements that a decolonized proprioception would allow us to feel.

Similarly, a colonized sense of balance stresses equilibrium, from economy to painting. A decolonial balance however includes the vestibular of falling down, of being fallen, of being held up by hands, propped up by hands. A decolonial balance is off its axis, elliptical, and spinning out of control. It lies down on others, with a rock for its pillow. I put internal in quotes because of course the term directs us to the idea of the personal interior, but this too is an effect of colonialism on interception. The great Guyanese poet Martin Carter for instance speaks of a 'university of hunger' – a common internal study that is extraindividual without succumbing to being sociological. But the awareness of something like breath or a heartbeat is only individuated in the process of colonialization and settlement, however ongoing. But perhaps most clearly in music, and black diasporic music most of all, we find centuries of resistance to this individuation of breath or heart, as not only countless lyrics but more tellingly countless beats, pauses, and rhythms testify. It is not just that we are without organs but that we are neither within nor without – our exteroception and interoception are all tangled up.

* * *

A similar thing goes on in Suely Rolnick's writing itself. Her writing is a micropolitical exercise. The continuous revision of these essays over time, under the influence of where she presents them as talks, and in collaboration with her conversations with students, presents us with a practice of writing that dissents from the completed argument, the scholarly object, and the establishment of intellectual private property. Rather than understanding these essays as a response to a particular macropolitical moment or condition, it might be fruitful to understand them as an untimely practice that goes on throughout *xviii*   Introduction

such moments and conditions, defending itself where it must, but refusing to be identified in the terms of these macropolitical threats or demands. One way she is able to do this is to remain in resonance with other kinds of practices, the ongoing insurgencies which similarly will not identify themselves. This resonance is not a representation but a commitment to extraentanglement.

Here I am reminded of one of Felix Guattari's discussions of Freud. Guattari speaks of two Freuds. One was the Freud who 'discovered' the unconscious. This is the Freud of dreams, slips, jokes, and the uncanny. This is the Freud who reads and narrates the unconscious and falls back into wonder at its infinite ability to produce symptoms. The other Freud is the scientist who moves toward the id-ego-superego schematic and toward various developmental theories to try to frame this unconscious in consciousness. Guattari marvels at Freud's ability to hold the scientist at bay for as much of his thinking as he did, and to risk the resonance of the unconscious reverberating into a revolt of the unconsciousnesses. This particular discussion I am thinking about takes place in response to a question Guattari receives in an encounter in Brazil facilitated and written up by Suely Rolnick and published in the seminal *Molecular Revolution in Brazil*. This was a book enacted and composed in the last days of the Brazilian dictatorship, published the first years of the return to civilian rule, and whose influence then spirals for decades.

In a preface to one of the editions of *Molecular Revolution in Brazil*, Suely Rolnick writes that it was 'a book of many hands.' But one hand could be said to proliferate all the others, and that is the hand of Suely Rolnick. She talks about its profound impact, and she could be talking about me. My encounter with this book was both typical and untimely. It changed my thinking forever, years before I came to live in Brazil or to know it at all. Now as ever, ever as now, the urgency of Suely Rolnick's thinking into a history that is always contemporary is both welcome and necessary. The essays of Spheres of Insurrection will announce themselves where we need them most, even before we know we do!

26 November 2022

Prelude

Words Blooming Out of the Lumps in Our Throats

*The concept is the contour, the configuration, the constel-
lation of an event to come ... Every concept shapes and
reshapes the event in its own way. The greatness of a
philosophy is measured by the nature of the events to
which its concepts summon us ... Concepts are centers of
vibrations, each in itself and every one in relation to all the
others. This is why they all resonate rather than cohere or
correspond with each other.*

Gilles Deleuze and Félix Guattari[1]

This compilation brings together three of my essays from the
2010s. The first one was written in 2012, around the same time
that persistent signals began to emerge, emitted by the return
of all kinds of reactive forces hatching everywhere. At the time,
no one could have predicted that this return would end up
unleashing a global outbreak of fascism, an outbreak that's only
gotten worse.

2012 was the year when the Supremo Tribunal Federal (the
highest judiciary court in Brazil) began trials for prisoners
accused under to the so-called Mensalão scandal.[2] This was the
opening act in a strategy devised by reactive forces to assume
power, a strategy I refer to as a "new modality of the coup." In
the third essay in this book, this modality and the way it settles
into Brazilian society are approached as a kind of thriller, as a

xx Prelude

television series produced using the conventions of the thriller, broadcast by the news program with the largest national audience in Brazil. The episodes in this series are focused on corruption accusations against the government of then president Luiz Inácio da Silva (Lula), accusations that are intertwined with images that show cash flowing out of drainpipes, emphasizing the filthiness of everything denounced in the series. Presenting these real-life events in the form of a daily, televised spectacle and, more than anything, narrating them in the scandalous and twisted manner in which they were narrated (legitimated as neutral journalistic coverage), are ways of participating in the very construction of these events. These are, in other words, ways of participating in the very construction of the coup.

The new modality of the coup operates in the micropolitical sphere: the sphere corresponding to the regime of the unconscious proper to every political system. Both the politics of the production of subjectivity and the politics that guide desire and prevail in a political system are defined according to the regime of the unconscious particular to that system. Through these politics of desire and of subjectivation, a way of life is produced and reproduced; it gives existential consistency to a political system; without it, the system would be unable to sustain itself. It is important to add that the micropolitical sphere is also the sphere where lines of flight are drawn out of this regime of the unconscious, transfiguring it.

The goal of the micropolitical operations of the new modality of the coup is to create a subjective basis that can support the elimination of any barrier erected by national states against the interests of the new fold of capitalism (its financialized and neoliberal fold) in its rise to globalitarian[3] power, which began in the 1970s. Furthermore, what I'm describing here is the Brazilian version of the series that produced the new modality of the coup. This same series has been adapted in several other countries (especially in Latin America), the same way television series are adapted to different contexts when they're produced for different national audiences.

When this book was first published, in March 2018, the most popular episode of the Brazilian version of this thriller was the impeachment of then President Dilma Rousseff, which took place in 2016. This wasn't the last episode in the series. The kind of coup conceived and produced by means of this series, as part of its strategies, is not limited to the removal of a president, as was the case in traditional coups d'état. The script of the new modality of the coup begins long before the ousting of a president and extends far beyond it. Today, in 2022, as we prepare the publication of the English-language edition of this book, we are witnessing the release of a new season of this same thriller, a season focused on the outbreak of the fascist plague. This outbreak (which was deliberately brought about by events included in the first season of the series) went totally out of control, beyond anything envisaged in the script of the series, spreading through the social body faster and faster with each passing day.

The second and third essays in this book were written between 2016 and 2018, in the heat of the planetary rise to power of reactive fascist forces everywhere. By contrast, and against the brutality of the events featured in this thriller, these were also the years when we witnessed an intensification of a new kind of political resistance that proliferated through various segments of Brazilian society. The first signals of this new kind of resistance emerged in 2013, emitted by a strand of the different forces stirred up during the sudden, mass protests that erupted all over the country. This same kind of resistance erupted elsewhere in Latin America during those same years.

New activists know about the need to act micropolitically, even if the goal is to bring about transformations in the macropolitical sphere. What new activists want is more than the necessary egalitarian distribution of rights sought out by macropolitical insurgency in the realm of the democratic state. What they demand is another kind of right, one that encompasses every other right: the right to exist fully – or, to be more precise, the right to life, to life as creating potency, as potency capable of creating transfigurations. This potency is the essence of life, of life in its active exercise, the kind of exercise that leads life to incarnate in new forms, every time life finds itself suffocated by the forms it embodies in the present. When this happens, when this process of creation and transfiguration takes place, life fulfills its ethical destiny. This is the necessary condition for life to persevere as an acting potency, for life to keep moving.

The goal of micropolitical resistance is the reappropriation of life's acting potency vis-à-vis its pimping[4] by the colonial-capitalistic regime, which leads this potency away from its

xxii Prelude

ethical destiny, reducing its capacity to act. New activists know (although not necessarily in a conscious way) that such pimping is what leads desire to submit to the perverse seduction of this regime, acting blindly and reactively. And if these new activists add the reappropriation of the vital potency to the goals of their insurrection, this is because they realize that the pimping of this potency is nothing less than the micropolitical principle of the colonial-capitalistic regime which now governs the whole planet. New activists know that this principle prevents desire from rising to the challenges that life (in its active exercise) imposes on us, and that this is what leads desire to guide its choices and actions in the direction of the accumulation of capital (not just economic and political capital but also social and political capital, which is inextricable from narcissistic capital, the accumulation of which guides the kind of subject produced by this regime as it directs its existence).

The struggle to transform the micropolitical principle that directs the actions of desire is different than the struggle to transform power relations in the macropolitical sphere. Micropolitical struggle does not follow a pre-established program, and it does not have pre-established goals. It also does not require organized movement, as is the case with macropolitical struggle (having a program, a goal, and an organization is what justifies the use of the term "militance," with its connotations of soldiers and a military, in reference to macropolitical activism). Rather, micropolitical struggle operates as a series of processes of collective experimentation that take place right here and right now, with the intention of creating new forms of existence. This entails emancipating desire from its subjection to the colonial-capitalist system. And these are the processes capable of transforming the micropolitical principle of production and reproduction of the type of society and the type of subjectivity corresponding to the colonial-capitalistic system. In other words, these are the processes capable of transforming the regime of the unconscious that is dominant under this system.

The new kind of insurrection, guided as it is by a micropolitical perspective, is embraced with notable vigor by the younger generations, especially by those living on the margins of major urban centers and by those belonging to other stigmatized social groups (those suffering from the stigma of race, class, sexuality, gender, etc.).[5] The effects that the forces pulsating

Prelude   *xxiii*

in these movements have on my body are certainly among the factors that set in motion the writing of the second essay included in this volume.

Convulsive periods are always the hardest to live through, but they are also the moments when life screams loudest. These screams are a kind of alarm call that life sets off to awaken us and to call us into action for the purpose of bringing balance back to it. This same alarm call, though, can also bring about the opposite effect, causing us to respond reactively. In the specific case of the colonial-capitalistic world, both responses tend to be intense. This is because the regime of the unconscious that directs the production of existence corresponding to this world is the pimping of life, which tends to turn us into zombies. This is a condition from which we all suffer to a greater or lesser extent. It is especially violent in the regions of the world razed by European colonial enterprises. But these periods are also times when the vital alarm can reach those who are now in a state of coma brought about by the regime, those of who have not entirely given themselves over to abuse, those who can still act in a way that breaks with their zombie condition, those who can rise to the challenge of what life demands from them.

In the current fold of capitalism (financialized and neoliberal), pimping technologies have increased their precision and efficacy. Desire is perversely seduced in increasingly violent and refined ways. This leads desire to be subjected to its own abuse with increasing jouissance. The high degree of expropriation of life (not just human life) that follows from this, which is exacerbated by the current economic crisis, triggers life's alarm call, making it ring loudly and stridently. Faced with this alarm (an exasperated vital scream), a new kind of activism emerges, which mobilizes those who were already in the process of freeing themselves from their zombie condition, and who can now move forward with that process in a faster and more intense way.

The irruption of processes of experimentation, characteristic of this new form of activism, is an active response to the alarm raised by life. This response emerges from a desire that has broken free from the spell of seduction cast by colonial-capital-istic pimping. Once it is free from this the spell, desire redirects its actions, and it seeks to place itself in the service of the preser-vation of life. This is why affects related to moments such as the ones we are now experiencing remain inscribed in our memories.

xxiv   Prelude

It is the reason why these affects serve as the principal compass that guides desire every time desire falls back into reactivity.

Each of the essays here included was published and presented in public lectures, in several languages, and in different contexts. They've been written and rewritten countless times. Every time I revisited them, I reworked them in order to address imprecisions that revealed themselves in the process of translation, or in readings completed by different interlocutors,[6] or in conversation with the audiences present in the different venues where they were presented (this is particularly true of the classroom, of the regular and collective dialogue I enjoy with students). The need to rewrite these essays also came from the urgencies different moments brought to my spirit, producing lumps in my throat which demanded the reformulation of certain concepts in ways that could embody what those urgencies brought about. At other times, I reworked these essays incorporating ideas that emerged from other texts I've written during the same period, moved by other, different urgencies that pressed upon my spirit, producing other lumps in my throat.

What you have in your hands, then, is the most recent version of these essays, prepared for this English-language version. I reformulated some passages and added some notes, either to clarify facts or concepts or to underline matters unfolding in 2018, when the book was first published in Portuguese. That said, I have kept intact the traces of time inscribed in its first edition: not just the traces of its historical juncture but also the traces of the stage of elaboration certain concepts had in my writing at that time, in that particular moment of my continuous process of elaboration. I chose to leave these marks because they serve as indicators of the limits of what is thinkable in the face of the initial manifestations of what we now understand as a return of the fascist plague, adapted for a new context.

In light of this process of continuous elaboration, readers will note that certain words, phrases, and even whole paragraphs appear more than once in all three essays: veritable obsessions. Each repetition, however, unfolds in new directions, expanding the sense of what is repeated or rendering its meaning more precise. Among these repetitions (which I deliberately chose to maintain) there are slight modifications, at times almost imperceptible. They result from the need to refine the way I listen to the overtones and undertones of embryonic words when I look

Prelude

xxv

to embody the affect generated by the experience of the events that led me to rewrite these essays in the first place. This need requires a search for words that are increasingly in tune with these affects, in order to bring them into existence, allowing them to enter the social scene. Once present in that scene, the affect embodied in such words can enter into compositions with other words that result from the innumerable and infinitely variable modulations of the affect corresponding to these same events (the modulations produced by other persons, from different social segments, and from different parts of the planet). Our actions make possible the transformation of the sinister landscape that now defines our current moment.

For the Guarani, the need to refine our way of listening to the overtones and undertones of embryonic words is an obvious need, and their language makes this clear. The Guarani word for "throat" is *ahy'o*, but it can also be *ñe'e raity*, a compound term made of two words: *ñe'e* ("soul-word," the Guarani term for what the English designates simply as "word") and *raity* (which means "nest"). *Ñe'e raity* can thus be translated, quite literally, as "place where the soul-words nest."[7] The Guarani use this compound term because they know that embryonic words form whenever our bodies are fertilized by the spirit of our time, thanks to our interactions with the forces that animate the environmental, social, and mental ecosystem. When all this happens, and only when this happens, words have a soul: either the soul of worlds in their current form or the soul of embryonic events, of nestlings in our throats, the presence of which brings tension to those worlds.

For the Guarani, that words have souls and that the soul needs to find its words is something so fundamental that their very understanding of the cause of disease is always defined by the separation of word and soul (this is true for physiological as well as spiritual diseases, the kind we, white Western subjects, refer to as "mental illnesses"). This indicates that, for the Guarani, the contraction between word and soul at the heart of the term *ñe'e* is always a virtual contraction. It may be actualized, or it may not, and for it to be actualized it must be exercised. The Guarani also know that there is an appropriate time for the germination of these embryonic futures, and that, for this germination to take place, the nest of words must be cared for appropriately.

xxvi   Prelude

To rise to the spirit of our times; to be up to the challenges life imposes on us every time it suffocates; to feel the pulse of the embryonic words generated by these demands (words nesting in our throats), and to look after this nest; to stay attuned to the temporality necessary for the germination of these event-words, so as to name – as precisely as possible – what it is that blooms in the face of this suffocation, in order to bring it into existence, bringing breath back to life, allowing it to regain its balance: Isn't this what the practice of thought should aspire to be? Isn't this precisely the micropolitical potency of the act of thinking? Doesn't this characterize and guarantee the ethics of thought? More broadly, isn't this, in the end, what defines the singularity of a life?

I hope these essays help readers find, in their own bodies, a few resonances of the affects mobilized by the forces that agitate the present, the affects that announce new events with them. I also hope that these resonances help them dissolve the lumps in their throats whenever their throats are pregnant with embryonic futures that begin to nest there. I hope, lastly, that the process of dissolving these lumps brings about the germination of words or other signs that carry with them modulations of a future – the future nesting in our bodies – modulations that remain beyond the reach of these essays.

In sum, and above all, I hope this book constitutes a small contribution to the collective creation of new scenarios capable of dissipating the brutality of the present, new scenarios that can bring life back to us: a life less pimped, freed from the perverse seduction to which we are all subjected. Scenarios that allow us to dissolve as much as possible the lumps in our throats, before these lumps turn malignant, metastasizing and spreading all over the social body. This is the sense, the meaning, of this book.

Suely Rolnik, May 2022

Colonial-Capitalistic Unconscious

We're writing for unconsciousnesses that have had enough. We're looking for allies. We need allies. And we think these allies are already out there, that they've gone ahead without us, that there are lots of people who've had enough and are thinking, feeling, and working in similar directions: it's not a question of fashion but of a deeper "spirit of the age" informing converging projects in a wide range of fields.

Gilles Deleuze and Félix Guattari[8]

A sinister atmosphere shrouds our planet. The ambient air, saturated by the toxic particles of the colonial-capitalistic regime, is suffocating us. Through successive transmutations, this regime has persisted and grown more and more sophisticated since its founding in the late fifteenth century. Its contemporary version – financialized, neoliberal and globalitarian – began to take shape in the transition from the nineteenth to the twentieth century, intensifying after World War I with the internationalization of capital. But it is only after the mid-1970s that this regime assumed its full power, affirming itself decisively – and not coincidentally – after the micropolitical movements that shook the planet in the 1960s and 1970s. During those years, and particularly in the mid-1970s, a process of discernment began. It seeks to decipher the current paths pursued by the regime in all its complexity, which includes the principles that govern it and the elements that create conditions for its consolidation.

And yet, as is often the case during times of radical transition, it is only later (after the mid-1990s, when the disastrous effects of this regime are more clearly felt in everyday life) that this process of discernment expands and refines itself, giving way to a collective debate that has been unfolding ever since. This debate is propelled by the experience of social movements that emerged over the course of the 1980s as a reaction to the current regime's rise to power. When toxic clouds form in the densifying atmosphere in one of the regions under the domain of globalitarian capitalism, each time its perversion exceeds the limits of the tolerable, social movements cut through the skies of this regime, like lighting.

The intensity of this irruption, comparable to the violence of the regime that unleashed it, tends to temporarily disturb the regime's tyrannical omnipotence. And as quickly as these irrupting movements appear, they fade away, only to reappear later, in different ways and in different places, mobilized by newly suffocating events, which in turn lead these movements to produce other cartographies, other senses, different from those that precede them. This series of movements extends into the early 2000s,[9] at which point the series was interrupted, resuming later after the crisis of 2008.[10] The new series of movements, still running its course today, arose in different parts of the planet, especially after the early 2010s.

This essay is embedded in the context of those movements and of the debate they unleashed. Its point of departure is one of the questions on the agenda of the collective construction signaled by those movements: the nature of the relationship between capital, on the one hand, and vital force, on the other, that corresponds to the regime in its current version (which is entirely different from its previous one, Fordism). In this new version, the domain of vital force from which capitalism feeds is no longer reduced to its expression as a workforce. This implies a radical metamorphosis of the very notion of work, a transformation which gradually dilutes the democratic constitutional state and the labor laws corresponding to the Fordist version of the capitalist regime.[11]

The Abuse of Life

As is well known, the central operation of the capitalist economy is the exploitation of the workforce and of the cooperation intrinsic to production. Its purpose is extracting surplus value. We can refer to this operation as a form of "pimping," to use a word that more precisely names the frequency of the vibration of its effects on our bodies. This operation has changed along with the different metamorphoses of the regime over the course of the five centuries of its existence. In its new version, it is life itself that capital appropriates. More precisely, what the regime appropriates is the essence of life, its potency of creation of new forms, at the exact moment that the impulse of this potency emerges. In other words, what gets pimped by capitalism is the germinating potency of life itself. The regime also appropriates the cooperation on which this potency depends for the germination of life to be completed. The vital force of creation and cooperation is thus channeled by capitalism towards the construction of a world conceived according to its objectives.

The drive to create, individually and collectively, new forms of existence; the functions of this drive and its codes, its representations: this is what the new version of capitalism exploits, transforming it into its source of propulsion. What follows is that the source from which the regime extracts its force is not merely economic but also, intrinsically and indissociably, cultural and subjective, if not ontological, which grants it a perverse power, more expansive, more subtle, and more difficult to counteract.

Faced with this scenario, it is evidently not enough to act in the macropolitical sphere, where the whole spectrum of the political left traditionally acts, especially the institutionalized segment of it (this explains their impotence vis-à-vis the current courses pursued by capitalism). According to the vision introduced by authors who have worked through the new relationship between capital and work by focusing on the appropriation of the potency of creation by capital – authors such as Toni Negri and Michael Hardt,[12] who designated the regime's new fold as "cognitive capitalism" – resistance today consists of an effort of collective reappropriation of that potency in order to build what the authors call "the common."[13]

4 Colonial-Capitalistic Unconscious

If we take this concept a bit further, we can define the common as the immanent field of the life drive of a social body when it takes this drive into its own hands, in a way that steers it towards the creation of modes of existence that can embody what demands to come through. Moreover, according to Hardt and Negri, changes in the forms of reality emerge from the construction of the common. Their argument is that if, on the one hand, during industrial capitalism, the forms of the workforce and their cooperation – in this case, organized as an assembly line – were pre-defined by capital, in the mode of expropriation of that drive proper to the new version of the regime, its forms are not predetermined, because what capital appropriates is precisely the potency of the construction of these forms. Even though, according to Hardt and Negri, this opens the possibility of autonomy in the guidance of the life drive, this drive is nonetheless diverted in favor of the production of settings for the accumulation of capital.

Furthermore, according to the authors, and assuming the vital potency belongs to those who work, it is precisely the experience of its relative autonomy that creates conditions favorable to its reappropriation. Resuming our dialogue with them, we may add that it is based on a desire-driven, individual and cooperative reappropriation of the ethical destiny of the vital drive[14] – that is, on its ontological reappropriation – that a collective rerouting of this drive (away from its abuse by capitalism) can take place in the direction of an ethics of existence. And yet, as Hardt and Negri point out, its reappropriation by society remains virtual so long as it does not find its forms of actualization. The search for these forms depends on a collective will to act towards the construction of the common, which is not given *a priori*.

It is precisely in that direction that some of the collective movements I reference above (which erupted in the mid-1990s and have burst onto the scene at different moments ever since) have been moving, in activism and, not coincidentally, in art (the borders that separate activism and art have become less and less discernible). In this transterritoriality, favorable conditions are created both for the mobilization of the potency of creation of activism and for the micropolitical potency of artistic practices. Despite having their essence precisely in that potency, artistic practices now tend to find themselves destitute of it, pimped as

Colonial-Capitalistic Unconscious

they are in the service of capital, which makes the domain of art a privileged source of expropriation.

A sense of restlessness drives the writing of this essay. Though we take an important step forward when we recognize, like the authors cited above, that it isn't enough to resist the current regime macropolitically, and that it's also necessary to act towards reappropriating the force of creation and cooperation – which is to say that it's also necessary to act micropolitically – to recognize this rationally does not guarantee effective actions in that direction. In fact, the reappropriation of the drive to creation is only effectuated when it guides the actions of desire in such a way that it imprints upon them their direction and their mode of relating to the other.

These kinds of actions, however, tend to crash against the barrier of the politics of production of both subjectivity and desire inherent to the current regime. As in any other regime, the mode of subjectivation produced in it is what gives the regime its existential consistency, without which it could not sustain itself. The two go hand in hand. In the case of the new fold of the colonial-capitalistic regime, the abuse of the life drive prevents us from recognizing this drive as ours, which makes its reappropriation something less obvious than reason would hope for. In light of this, we clearly cannot take back the reins of that potency by a simple edict of the will, imperious as the will may be. Nor can we reclaim it by means of consciousness, regardless of how lucid or well intentioned consciousness is. It is also not possible to collectively reappropriate that potency as one single, supposedly natural body, allegedly given *a priori*, and, furthermore, we cannot do this in absolute synergy with all the elements that constitute this body (these are the pretensions of the messianic harbingers of paradise on Earth).

Resistance must take place in the very field constituted by the politics of the production of subjectivity and desire dominant in the regime in its contemporary version, which is another way of saying that resistance must take place in the regime that dominates within us. This is not something that will fall in our laps like some gift from heaven, and neither is it something we will find in some promised land. On the contrary, this is a territory that must be tirelessly conquered and constructed in every human existence that comprises a society, and it necessarily involves its relational universe. In this mode of resistance, temporary communities are formed, within which conditions for the construction of the common emerge. These communities, however, never occupy the social body as a whole, for this body is made and unmade in the relentless clash between different types of forces.

But How to Free life from its Pimping?

To rise in revolt in this territory implies a diagnosis of the standing mode of subjectivation and of the regime of the unconscious proper to it. It also requires us to find out where and how to make viable a displacement of the principle that governs this regime. Without this work, the much lauded call for the collective reappropriation of the creative force (as a form of prevention against the pathology of the present) will always remain confined to the laboratory of ideas. It will run the risk of remaining confined to the plane of the imaginary, confined to its pleasant and encouraging illusions – capturing devices in and of themselves.

I propose the term "colonial-capitalistic unconscious" to designate the politics of the unconscious that is dominant in this regime and that runs throughout its history, shifting nothing but its modalities together with its transmutations and its forms of abuse of the vital force of creation and cooperation. In that sense, we can also refer to this politics as a "pimp colonial-capitalistic-unconscious," for the reasons outlined above. More likely than not, the resistance to that regime of the unconscious is what Deleuze and Guattari had in mind when they called for a protest of the unconciousnesses in 1972, when the work of collectively elaborating the bold experience of May 1968 was just dawning and, simultaneously, when the rise to power of the new regime was sending its first, still nebulous signals.

The intent behind the present text is to probe the current modality of the pimp-colonial unconscious introduced by financialized and neoliberal capitalism, which is defined, I insist, by the abduction of the creating force at the very source of its world-germinating impulse. But how to dodge this regime of the unconscious within ourselves and in our surroundings? In other words, what are the protests of the unconsciousnesses proposed by Deleuze and Guattari? Answering this question demands a kind of research involving our own subjective experience. We must look within ourselves for access points to the potency of creation: the source of the drive-movement that guides the actions of desire in its various destinies. This is a work of experimentation on the self that demands constant attention. In this kind of research, the formulation of ideas is inseparable from a process of subjectivation where the reappropriation of this potency becomes possible for brief and fleeting moments, moments that gradually become longer, more frequent, and more consistent as we move forward with this work.

Thus, the work required to answer this question demands that two shifts take place at the same time: on the one hand, a shift in the politics of the production of subjectivity and of desire (dominant in the new version of Western, modern, colonial-capitalistic culture); on the other hand, a shift in the politics of thought production proper to that culture. For that to happen, we must activate the vital core of thought and its ability to undo the configurations of power. Without that, our intention is dead on arrival. From the perspective of those shifts, to think and to rise in insurgency turn into one and the same practice. Neither can advance without the other.

The fact that this practice of thought cannot take place in isolation (though it must take place, as a matter of principle, within the context of each existence) corroborates the inextricability of thought and insurgency. Thought simply cannot take place in isolation, for two reasons. First, because the engine of thought neither begins nor ends in the individual. It does not begin in the individual because its origin resides in the effects that the forces of the world have on each of the bodies that make up that world. And it does not end in the individual because its products are forms of expression of those forces that result in singularizing processes, which are molded in a field common to all and transfigured by all. This has nothing to do with self-reflexivity, interiority, or private matters. The second reason why thought does not take place in isolation is that the exercise of thought feeds from resonances of other efforts made in the same direction and from the collective force that these resonances promote – not just through their power of pollination but also and mostly due to the synergy they produce.

Resonances of this type are found not only in academic disciplines that sometimes claim a monopoly of expertise on the matter, disciplines such as critical theory, cultural studies, post-colonial studies, critical race and ethnicity studies, women's studies, or queer studies. We can find these resonances in various fields of theoretical practice and, furthermore, they also emerge from thought production in different domains of everyday experience: from so-called high culture to popular music to the kind of experimentation that happens in domains such as sexuality, romantic relationships, food culture, etc. These resonances can also (and mostly) be found in that which indigenous and Afro-descendant people have insistently told us, something that's been ringing loud and clear for everyone except those who don't want to pay attention, or those too numb to pay attention. These resonances and the synergies they produce create conditions for the formation of a common, collective body with a potency of invention that acts in singular and variable ways and that can curb the power of the forces that prevail in other constellations (those that are made up of bodies that try to pimp out the life drive of other bodies, or that make themselves available to be pimped by others).

With those synergies in place, paths open, and they reroute this vital potency away from its destructive destiny. This is precisely the perspective that governs thought in the writing of this essay – a perspective that is thus, and as a matter of principle, not just transdisciplinary but also inextricably linked to a clinical-political pragmatics. Because this is necessarily the work of each and all of us, and because this work is never-ending, the ideas shared here amount to no more than a few conceptual tools among the many being forged today, in multiple directions, in response to the question posed above: how to free life from its pimping?

Such a process of invention is the result of a collective intelligence activated at exponentially higher speeds, mobilized by the urgency of confronting the high degree of perversion of capitalism in its new version. The tools suggested here will help us examine the current regime's politics of the production of subjectivity, of desire, and of thought, as well as the relationship with the other, a production that leads us to blindly consent to the appropriation of the force of creation by capital. These tools will also help us examine the politics that make viable the reappropriation of this force. We will thus have a criterion to distinguish between the two perspectives that govern practices

Colonial-Capitalistic Unconscious 9

in the micropolitical sphere and between the formations of the unconscious in the social field that result from each one of these perspectives.

In order to make evident the basic differences between these two perspectives – these micropolitics – I'll draw on Lygia Clark. I'll do so because this Brazilian artist invented a profusion of "propositions" (as she herself called those practices) that enhance, in those willing to try them, the access both to their own potency of creation and to the activation of the work needed to reappropriate this potency, making its abuse as unfeasible as possible. Clark's propositions provide opportunities to launch into a process that helps us dodge the power of the colonial-capitalistic unconscious in our own subjectivity. At the very least, they legitimize and strengthen this process wherever it is already underway. I'll focus only on *Caminhando* (*Walking*), the first such proposition by Clark and the one that gave rise to her other, related propositions. This work will provide us with the basis for what I intend to explore here.

Walking with Lygia Clark, on the Topological Surface

Caminhando (*Walking*) dates to 1963. Its creation is a singular response to one of the challenges propelling artistic practices produced in the 1960s and 1970s: how to activate the clinical-political potency of art, its micropolitical potency, which was weakened at the time by its neutralization in the art system. The impulse that triggered this movement has its origins in a long process first unleashed by the avant-gardes of the early twentieth century, whose inventions spread and sprouted all throughout the fabric of society in a process interrupted only by the two world wars. After the end of World War II, this sprouting resumed its course in a more radical and denser way until it generated the expansive social movement that shook the planet from the 1960s until the mid-1970s, a movement marked by the reappropriation of the creative drive in collective practices of everyday life, far beyond the restricted field of art.

The origin of Clark's proposition was a study for a work of art that she would later (and not coincidentally) name *The Before is the After* (*O antes é o depois*). With that study, a new path opened for her *Bichos*, her well-known series of sculpture-like works, a path towards the exploration of the Möbius strip: a one-sided topological surface where every point on the strip can be traced continuously to any other point on it, rendering what apparently seems like two sides into one and the same side, one and the same surface.

In her study for that work, the artist researched successive, longitudinal cuts on the surface of a Möbius strip made from a piece of paper. As her research moved forward, Clark realized that an odd experience took place in the very instant of the act of cutting. Slowly, the artist discerned what that experience revealed to her: the work as such is realized in the act of cutting and in the experience promoted by cutting, and not in the object that results from it. This experience consists in the emergence of another way of seeing and feeling time and space. According to Clark, this is a time without a before and without an after, a space with no frontside and no backside, no inside or outside, no up, no down, no left, no right. Furthermore, the becoming of the shape of the strip, which takes place each time the cutting makes its way across its surface, brings about the experience of a time immanent to the act of cutting. This other way of seeing and feeling provides, therefore, access to the experience of a space that does not precede the act of cutting but results from it, and which thus cannot be dissociated from time. In sum: when experienced from the perspective of Clark's proposition,

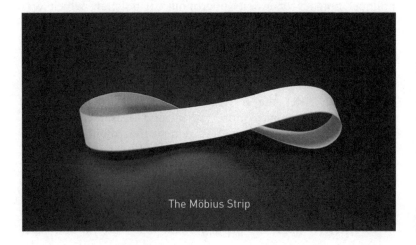
The Möbius Strip

space emerges from the becoming of the forms that are created in the topological surface of the strip, the products of the acts of cutting.

Make Your Own Walking

The revelation left Lygia Clark perplexed. It led her to turn this experience into an art proposition, which she named *Caminhando* (*Walking*). It consists in offering to the public strips of paper, scissors, and glue, along with short, simple instructions

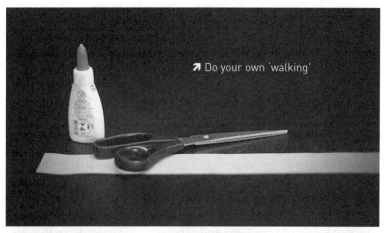

↗ Do your own 'walking'

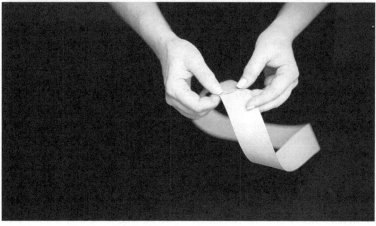

12 Colonial-Capitalistic Unconscious

and a single warning: every time the act of cutting reaches a spot on the surface of the strip previously having been cut through, this spot must be avoided to allow the cutting to continue.

Those willing to experience her proposal are asked to use the kind of materials chosen by Clark to make their own Möbius strip, by twisting the paper strip and gluing together one end of it to the reverse side of the other end. One must then choose any point on the surface to begin cutting it lengthwise. As the cutting continues, and if Clark's instructions are heeded (i.e., no cutting through a previously cut point), the strip of paper gets more and more narrow. Eventually, the strip of paper gets too narrow. When this point is reached, if we keep cutting, we split the strip in two, which turns each of the resulting strips into regular, two-sided strips of paper.

Surely, the artist did not issue her instructions in vain. On the contrary, the very possibility of the work happening depends on following these instructions, particularly the warning to avoid cutting through the same, previously perforated spot. The act of cutting is not a neutral act: its effects vary according to the type of cut that each one chooses in their own "walking." If we follow the artist's instructions and cut around a previously cut spot, and if we do this every time we go around, a difference will be produced in the form of the strip and in the space created from this form. The form will gradually multiply in a process of constant variation which is exhausted only when there is no more surface to cut. The work is effectuated in the repetition of the act that creates difference. It begins and it ends in this act. The work itself, in sum, is the event of that experience.

If, on the other hand, we don't follow the artist's instructions and we cut through a part of the strip that has already been cut, the Möbius splits into two circles and their form becomes static, always identical to itself. The act implied in this kind of cut is a sterile act; it does not produce a work. In other words, it does not produce the event of creation of a difference where the work itself takes shape.

But what does this have to do with reappropriating the potency of creation? More generally speaking, what does this have to do with shifting away from the politics of the production of subjectivity governed by the pimp-colonial unconscious, which makes viable the expropriation of this potency? To answer

Colonial-Capitalistic Unconscious

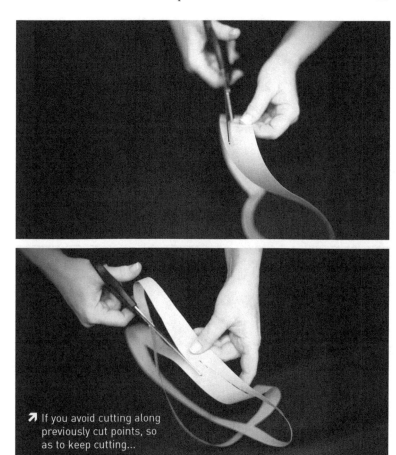

↗ If you avoid cutting along previously cut points, so as to keep cutting...

Colonial-Capitalistic Unconscious

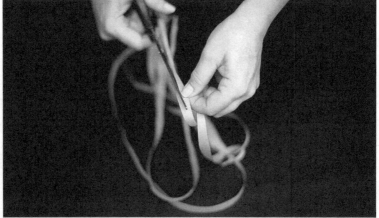

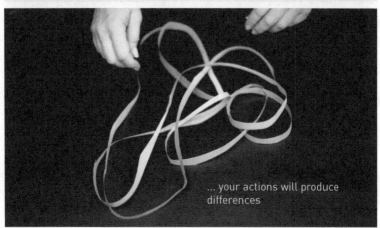

... your actions will produce differences

Colonial-Capitalistic Unconscious

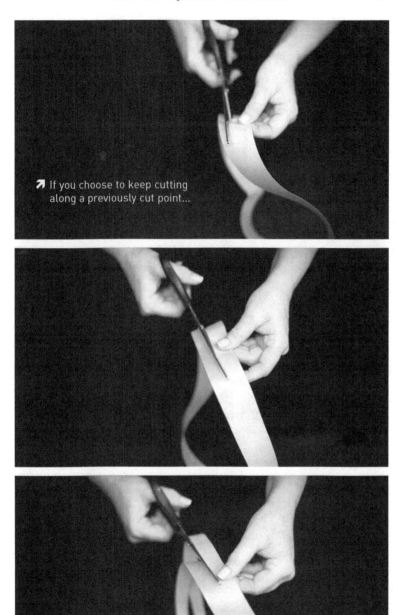

↗ If you choose to keep cutting along a previously cut point...

16 Colonial-Capitalistic Unconscious

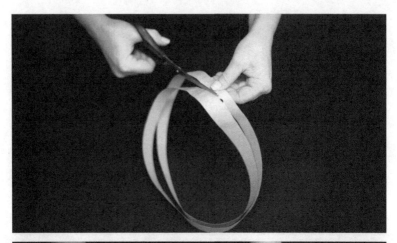

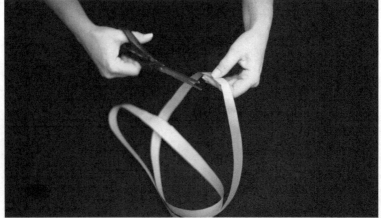

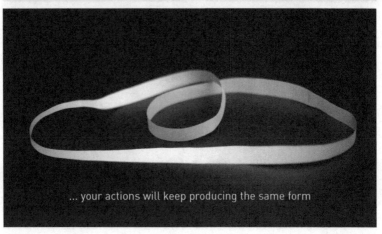

... your actions will keep producing the same form

these questions, we must examine the experience where this proposition is actualized as a work event. We must, above all, examine both the choice of action that makes this experience possible and the difference that distinguishes it from those that preclude it.

With this intention, I offer you, dear reader, an exercise for the imagination: picture a Möbius strip projected onto the skin of the world and imagine this skin as a topological surface composed of all kinds of bodies (human and nonhuman) in various and variable connections, which allows us to describe this surface as "relational-topological." Imagine, too, that one of the faces of this surface corresponds to the present forms of the world, where the vital forces that animate the world are molded. Imagine that the other face corresponds to the vital forces themselves in relation to the other forces that compose a world ecosystem in its actuality. Imagine, furthermore, that, just like in a Möbius strip, these two faces are inseparable, constituting one and the same surface, one and the same side.

In fact, there is no form that isn't the concretization of the vital flux. Reciprocally, there is no force that isn't either molded in some form (which produces the existential sustenance of that form) or in the process of molding itself into new configurations (which produces a metamorphosis of the current forms, or even their dissolution, in a process of continuous differentiation). With this in mind, let us first examine how it is we apprehend forms and forces respectively, the types of experiences these capacities of apprehension promote, and the dynamics of the relationship between them.

Forms and Forces: A Paradoxical Relationship

Just as forms and forces are different, so too are the faculties by means of which we register their respective signals. Exerting these faculties gives rise to two of the multiple dimensions of that complex experience we call "subjectivity." And just as forms and forces, although distinct, are inextricable (two faces constituting one and the same topological-relational surface of a world), these faculties also operate simultaneously and inseparably, in the relational plot that holds bodies together in each passing moment. This is the case regardless of whether we are conscious of these faculties or not, and regardless of the degree to which we keep each one of them active as guides in our choices and in the actions deriving from these choices.

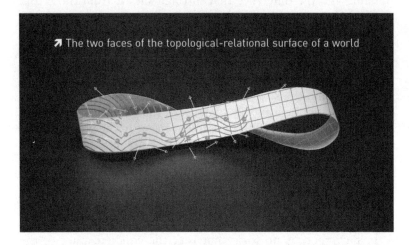

↗ The two faces of the topological-relational surface of a world

The signals emitted by the forms of a world are picked up by means of perception (sense experience) and feeling (the experience of psychological emotion). These faculties make up the most immediate experience we have of a given world. Through this experience, we apprehend a world in its concreteness and its current outlines – what we designate as reality. They are modes of existence, articulated according to sociocultural codes that

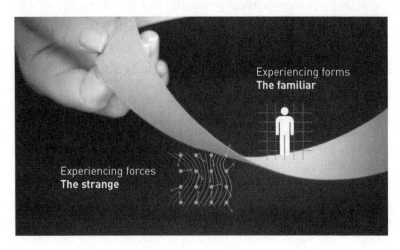

Experiencing forms
The familiar

Experiencing forces
The strange

configure different characters and their distribution in the social field, as well as their respective representations. This comes hand in hand with a certain distribution of access to material and immaterial goods.

The cartography of a world is defined by all these elements: elements of a world in its concreteness. These cartographies and their codes orient the mode of apprehension of the faculties referenced above: when we see, hear, smell, taste, or touch something, our perception and our feelings already come linked to our repertoire of codes and representations, which we project onto the form of what we perceive or feel. This, in turn, allows us to attribute a meaning to it. This mode of apprehending a world, which I suggest we call "personal-sensory-sentimental-cognitive," produces our experience as "subjects," which is intrinsically linked to our sociocultural condition and shaped by its imaginary. Its function is to allow us to deal with social life: to decipher its forms, its codes, and its dynamics by means of perception, of cognition, and of information; to establish relationships with others by way of communication; and to feel those relationships in accordance with our psychological dynamic. In sum, deciphering the forms of a world is what makes possible our social existence.

As a matter of principle, this mode of apprehending a world is familiar to us, because it is set by cultural habits that guide us day to day. Yet in Western and Westernized societies, under the power of the colonial-capitalistic regime, the function of this capacity gains boundless power. The reason is that, in the politics of subjectivation dominant in these contexts, we tend to restrict ourselves to our experience as subjects, ignoring that, though this kind of experience is without a doubt indispensable – because it allows us to carry on with everyday life, with sociability, and with communication – it is not the only way of leading our existence; other, different ways of apprehending a world operate simultaneously. The reduction to this kind of experience is, precisely speaking, one of the core aspects of the mode of subjectivation operating under the rule of the colonial-capitalistic unconscious.

Let us now examine a way of apprehending a world that allows us to pick up the signals emitted by forces that animate that world and that bring about effects on our own body – "body" here understood in its condition as living being. Such

20   Colonial-Capitalistic Unconscious

effects result from the encounters we have – with people, things, landscapes, ideas, works of art, political situations or other kinds of situations, and so forth – whether these encounters take place in person, or via the technologies that make communication at a distance possible, or in any other way. These encounters bring about changes in the diagram of force vectors and of the relationships between them, producing various, new effects. Other ways of seeing and feeling emerge, ways we can associate with the experience Lygia Clark had as she cut her Möbius strip and which led her to create her *Walking*. Gilles Deleuze and Félix Guattari had a name for these other ways of seeing and feeling: they called them "percept" and "affect," respectively. Percept is different from perception, because it consists of an atmosphere that exceeds lived situations and their representations. Affect, on the other hand, must not be confused with affection, kindness, or tenderness, words that correspond to the common usage of the term "affect" in the Romance languages. What we are dealing with here is not psychological emotion; it is a "vital emotion" rendered by the meaning of the verb "to affect" – to touch, disturb, unsettle, move (a meaning which, on the other hand, is not usually expressed in noun form).

Percepts and affects have neither images, nor words, nor gestures, nothing that gives them expression. They are real, nonetheless, for they refer to that which is alive, within us and outside of us. They constitute an experience of appreciation for our surroundings that is more subtle, that functions as an extra-cognitive mode, a mode we might call "intuition." But, since this word can lead to misunderstandings,[15] I prefer to call it "body-knowing" or, better yet, "eco-ethological knowing" – the kind of knowing proper to any living being. An intensive kind of knowing, different from the sensory and rational knowledge proper to the subject.

This faculty, which I suggest we refer to as an "extra-personal-extrasensory-extrapsychological-extrasentimental-extracognitive" faculty, produces one of the experiences of the world that constitutes subjectivity: its experience "outside-the-subject," immanent to our condition as a living body (the body I've previously referred to as "resonant body" and which, more recently, I've began to call a "drive-body"). In this plane of subjective experience, we are constituted by the effects of the forces and their relationships, which agitate the vital flux of a world, and which singularly cross all the bodies that compose it, transforming all of them into one single body, in a state of constant variation, whether we are conscious of this or not. The function of this faculty is therefore to make possible our existence on that plane, which is immanent to all living beings among whom varying relationships are established, all of which composes a biosphere in a constant state of transmutation.

The means of relating to the other in this plane are different from communication, which is characteristic of the subject. For the time being, for lack of a more precise word, we can call this means of relating "resonance" or "reverberation." There is no distinction here between cognizant subject and exterior object. The other, human or nonhuman, is not something exterior, nor is it reduced to a mere representation that the subject projects onto it. In this plane, the world effectively lives in our body, generating (in our bodies) embryos of other worlds.

The pulse of the virtual worlds that beats inside our bodies throws us into a state of estrangement. This state intensifies in the Western and Westernized societies that now comprise practically the whole planet. This happens because the reduction of subjectivity to the experience of the subject (which characterizes the politics of subjectivation preponderant in these societies) entails a dissociation from our condition as living beings, which in turn separates us from affects and percepts and deprives us of the kind of knowing proper to any living being. Although the effects of the forces of the world on our bodies are stunning, the fact that our access to these effects is obstructed prevents us from apprehending them, which makes their beating pulse even more strange and disturbing to us. This is a second, essential aspect of the mode of subjectivation prevalent under the rule of the colonial-capitalistic unconscious regime, inseparable from its first aspect (the reduction of our experience of the world to our condition as subjects).

The Paradox That Triggers Desire

The experiences corresponding to each one of the faces of the topological-relational surface of the world function according to entirely disparate logics, scales, and speeds. Because they are

22   Colonial-Capitalistic Unconscious

simultaneous and inextricable, and because they are, at the same time, irreducible to each other, the dynamic between them is one not of opposition but of paradox. This dynamic, therefore, and as matter of principle, never results in any kind of synthesis (not even a dialectical one), and neither does it result in the domination or the nullification of one experience over the other (as promised by certain theories of cognitive and psychological development, more properly described as ideologies that undergird the rule of the subject, the rule proper to Western, modern, colonial-capitalistic culture). In short, the relationship between these experiences does not lead to any kind of permanent harmony or stability. On the contrary, it produces a constant tension that fluctuates only at the level of its intensity.

The virtual worlds engendered in the experience of forces produce a friction with the experience of forms molded according to the current sociocultural cartographies. The reason is simple: the fact that these cartographies are the embodiment of previous arrangements of forces (arrangements that are different from the present one, because they were produced by other bodies and from other connections between them) impedes the expression of the virtual worlds generated by the new arrangement of forces in the present. Subjectivity sees itself thrown into the experience of a state that is concomitantly strange and familiar, which destabilizes its outlines and the images it has of itself and of the world. This brings about a feeling of malaise, of being ill at ease.

A tension is thus generated between, on the one hand, the movement that pressures subjectivity to conserve the forms where life finds itself materialized and, on the other hand, the movement that pressures subjectivity to honor life in its germinating potency. Honoring this potency, and allowing for its exertion, allows for the embryos pulsating in the body to gain consistency in other forms of subjectivity and of the world; this compromises the current forms of the world. Stretched between these two movements (conservation and germination), subjectivity itself becomes a question mark, for which it will have to find an answer.

Let us refer to this tension-inducing question mark as the "drive-unconscious."[16] It is the engine that powers the processes of subjectivation. The beating pulse of a new problem triggers an alarm call that summons desire to act in order to restore a

Colonial-Capitalistic Unconscious

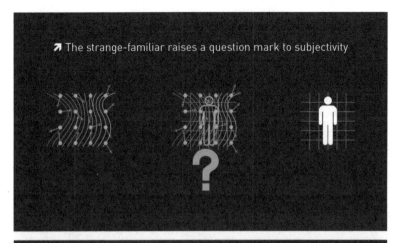

↗ The strange-familiar raises a question mark to subjectivity

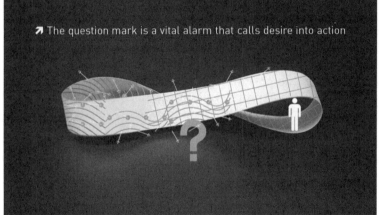

↗ The question mark is a vital alarm that calls desire into action

vital balance, which is also an existential and emotional balance. Desire is then impelled to cut through the relational-topological surface of the world, a cut that can bring back for subjectivity an outline and its meaning.

The moment desire is called upon to act is precisely the moment when its politics will be defined. These politics vary as a function of the different regimes of the drive-unconscious that orient them. To describe them, I suggest we return to the *Walking* Lygia Clark proposes to us, focusing on the two types of cut on the surface of the Möbius strip that this proposition invited us to consider.

Two Opposing Poles for the Politics of Desire: An Exercise in Fabulation

Now I invite you, dear reader, once again to engage in an exercise of fabulation. First, imagine the act of cutting projected onto the topological-relational surface of the world. Then, mindful that desire is what acts in us, imagine that the two possible types of cut in Clark's proposition correspond to two different politics of the actions of desire vis-à-vis the interrogation that set desire in motion to begin with (remembering that, as we saw in *Caminhando*, the choice of where and how we cut is not neutral, because the forms that will take shape on the topological surface depend on this choice). Imagine, then, that these two politics of desire occupy opposite ends of the vast and complex spectrum of micropolitics that guides desire's actions under the current regime. The clash between these opposite ends is what gives rise to the different destinies of reality: from the position where desire is most submissive to the regime of the colonial-capitalistic unconscious (the position that results, in theory, in a complete surrender to the expropriation of the force of creation), to the most deviating position (the one that would make possible the reappropriation of this force).

Evidently, these diametrically opposed positions are fictional figures; neither of them ever completely dominates the orientation

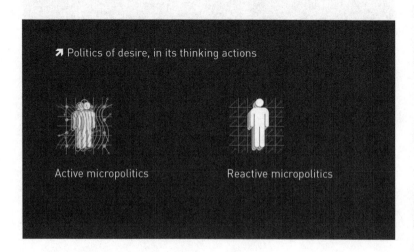

of desire, and neither exists in a pure state. We go back and forth between various positions or micropolitics, closer to or more distanced from an ethics of existence. These vary, in greater or lesser degree, with each passing moment and throughout the course of our lives. Likewise, the collective body fluctuates between various micropolitics predominant in each context and at each moment; it is formed by the clash of the different force vectors of the vital drive. In other words, much like subjects, the collective body does not remain identical to itself – much less stable – over time. This is so regardless of the position the collective body finds itself in: whether it is prone to the expropriation of the vital force, or whether it is in a place to resist this expropriation and invent other worlds and different unconscious regimes to direct its formations in the social field.

Let us now revisit the two different kinds of cuts available when considering Lygia Clark's *Walking*, and let's imagine, further, these cuts projected onto the surface of the world conceived as a Möbius strip. This will allow us to distinguish more clearly between, on the one hand, the essential characteristics of the micropolitics that have the potential power to escape the rule of the pimp-colonial-capitalistic unconscious and, on the other hand, the characteristics of those micropolitics that, on the contrary, lead us to surrender to that rule and to reproduce it in perpetuity. Drawing these distinctions will also allow us to explore the type of formations of the unconscious in the social field that result from each of these micropolitics.

Active Micropolitics and its Ethical Compass

Recall, first, the types of actions of desire that avoid cutting through previously chosen points, the kind of cuts performed in *Walking* when Clark's instructions are followed. Now imagine this type of cut being made on the topological-relational surface of a world, the surface where the acts of desire are performed. This politics of desire is proper to a subjectivity that inhabits the paradox of its two simultaneous experiences, as subject and as outside-the-subject. This is a subjectivity that can sustain itself in the tension that arises from the forces that emerge from both these experiences, which unleash the two paradoxical movements that constitute the drive-unconscious. Under this politics of desire,

26 Colonial-Capitalistic Unconscious

subjectivity can also stay attuned to the effects produced by the new diagrams of forces generated in the intensive experience of new encounters. This is a subjectivity that tolerates the turbulences caused by these encounters in its experience as subject – exactly the same turbulences that hurl it into a state of both strangeness and familiarity (what Freud called *unheimlich* and what is generally referred to as uncanniness).

In other words, what we're dealing with here is a subjectivity capable of supporting itself at the limit both of the language that structures it and of the disturbance that this experience brings to it: a subjectivity that withstands the tension that destabilizes it and that does so long enough to make possible the germination of a world, with its language and its senses. And if this subjectivity can support itself in this state of uncanniness, it is because it knows (extracognitively) without (cognitively) knowing that cutting through the surface at a point that has already been cut will not bring back balance to it, for it would keep it confined to a form that has lost its meaning, a form whose bankruptcy is responsible for its destabilization. In this case, what will guide desire in its cutting is the search for a response to the question that was posed to subjectivity when it saw itself stripped of its habitual parameters. Through its actions, desire will connect with unfrequented points on the topological-relational surface of a world in order to make its cuts, searching for paths that make possible the germination and the birth of the embryonic world that lives quietly inside the body.

Actualizing the seed of a world that lives in this subjectivity in a virtual state will result from the invention of something: an idea, an image, a gesture, a work of art, among other possibilities. It can also result from a new mode of existence, of sexuality, of eating, a new way of relating to the other, to work, to the state, or to any other element of the environment. Whatever it is, what matters is that what is invented carries with it the intensive pulse of the new ways of seeing and feeling generated by the effects of the web of relations between bodies (effects that are singular in each one of them) in such a way that it makes them sensible.

In other words, what matters in this politics of desire is transducing[17] affect or vital emotion (with its corresponding intensive qualities) into a sensible experience (regardless of the sphere of social life where this experience takes place, and regardless of its mode of expression) in such a way that this experience is

Colonial-Capitalistic Unconscious

inscribed onto the surface of the world, producing detours in its current architecture. Imagine, as you did in your experience with *Walking*, that, in making this type of cut, the initial form of the topological-relational surface of the world multiplies and differentiates along the way, in a continuous process of composition and recomposition. In this micropolitics, the acts of desire therefore consist in acts of creation that can inscribe the established existential territories and their corresponding cartographies, that can thus shatter the reassuring frame of the instituted.

In this case, the engine of desire, in its thinking acts, is the wish to preserve life itself in its essence – a will radically distinct from the one that wants to preserve the current cartography. However, the conservation of life does not happen separately from the forms currently on the surface of the world; it is based on a negotiation with these forms, in way that finds the points where desire can connect with the surface of the world to inscribe the cuts of the instituting force.

An ethical compass guides desire. Its needle points to the demands of life (in its insistence on enduring) every time life sees itself blocked from flowing through the cartography of the present. This compass guides the actions of desire towards the creation of difference; this is a response capable of effectively producing a new equilibrium for the vital drive, which depends on its ability to actualize the vital drive in new forms. This

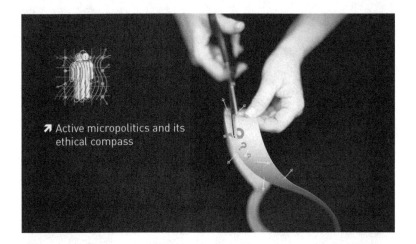

↗ Active micropolitics and its ethical compass

28 Colonial-Capitalistic Unconscious

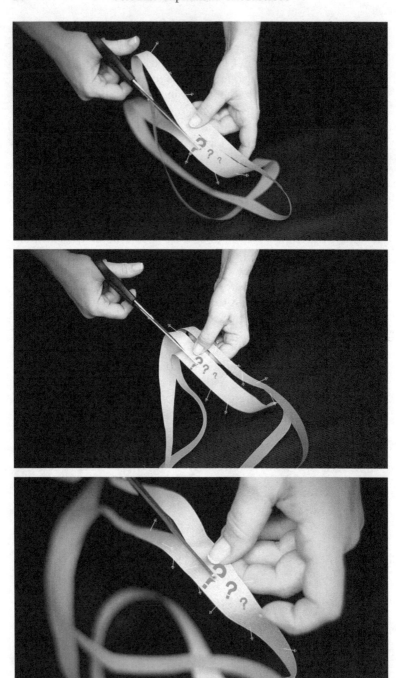

Colonial-Capitalistic Unconscious   29

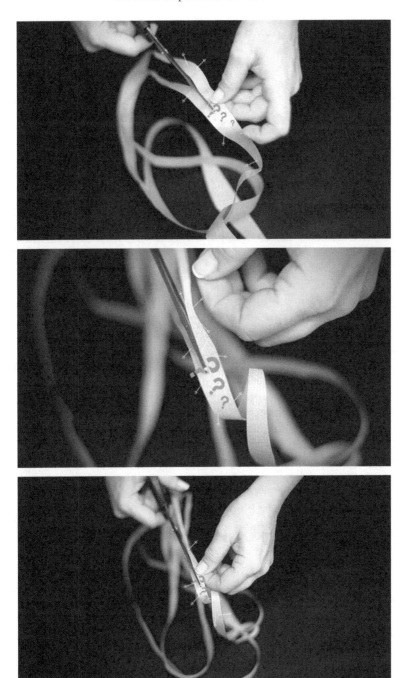

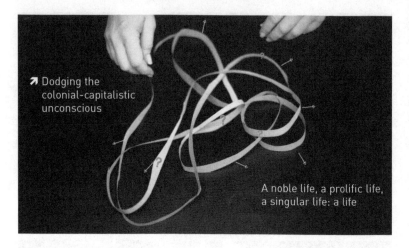

↗ Dodging the colonial-capitalistic unconscious

A noble life, a prolific life, a singular life: a life

is the nature of what we call an "event," which is produced by this kind of politics of desire: a becoming of subjectivity and, indissociably, a becoming of the relational fabric where subjectivity's turbulence and its impetus towards acting are generated.

Ruled by that micropolitics, desire lives up to its ethical function as an active agent in the creation of worlds. This politics of desire corresponds to a subjectivity that seeks to rise to the challenge of what happens to it. And if we expand the horizon of our gaze to include the surface of the world as it is configured today, we will see that an active micropolitics is proper to a life, individual or collective, that manages to reappropriate its potency and, with it, succeeds in dodging the power of the colonial-capitalistic unconscious that expropriates it. In short, a life that manages to be guided by an ethics of the drive. A noble life, a prolific life, a singular life: a life.

Reactive Micropolitics and its Moral Compass

I now ask you to imagine, dear reader, the kind of action on the surface of the relational-topological world corresponding to a desire that insists on cutting through previously chosen points (the kind of action taken in *Caminhando* when Clark's instructions are not followed). This type of cut corresponds

Colonial-Capitalistic Unconscious 31

to another fictional possibility, situated on one extreme end of the wide spectrum of potential micropolitics (the position most submissive to the pimp-colonial-capitalistic unconscious). Given that it is precisely this micropolitics that makes possible the expropriation of the drive-force of creation, let's break down its dynamics more carefully.

Unlike that other mode of subjectivation we just glimpsed, this politics of desire is proper to a subjectivity reduced to its experience as subject, a subjectivity whose horizon begins and ends in this experience. Because it is disconnected from its experience outside the subject, it can't decipher the effects of the forces that agitate a world in its condition as living being. The seed of a world that lives in this subjectivity is experienced by it as a body so strange and so inassimilable that it seems terrifying, which is why the effects of this presence will have to be neutralized at all costs and as soon as possible.

This kind of subjectivity experiences the universe as an object exterior to itself. It is only capable of deciphering it from the perspective of its experience as subject. The image of itself that results from this reduction is the image of an individual: an indivisible whole, as the term itself indicates. It is the image of what is believed to be a crystallized unit, separate from the other, which is also conceived as a presumably crystallized, individualized unit. This series of supposed units is thought to constitute the world, whose image – in the eyes of this subjectivity – is presumed to be a totality, equally crystallized and organized according to a stable distribution of fixed elements, with everything in its right place, everything equally fixed.

The image of a subjectivity eternally preserving the status quo (its own and the world's) is evidently a hallucinatory image. If this kind of preservation took place, it would stagnate the vital fluxes that animate the existence of both subjectivity and its world, which would ultimately spell their death. All this notwithstanding, what leads subjectivity to the belief in the mirage of preservation is the fear that the dissolution of the established world brings with it the dissolution of its own self. From the perspective of that type of subjectivity reduced to the subject and blurred with it, from the point of view of a subjectivity that sees itself mirrored in the cultural cartography that gives shape to it (as if it were the only world possible for it), the crumbling of *a* world is interpreted as a sign of the end of *the* world, and a sign

32 Colonial-Capitalistic Unconscious

of the end of subjectivity itself (or, in any case, what subjectivity sees as itself).

The fact is that, when subjectivity is reduced to the subject and blurred with it, it extracts its self-image from the reflection it gets from the current cultural cartography; it regards this reflection as the absolute and only image of itself. From that perspective, the crumbling of "a" world (the world shaped by the current cultural cartography) is interpreted as a sign of the end of "the" world, and the end of subjectivity itself (or what subjectivity believes to be its one and only self). When the tension between the strange and the familiar brings this sense of danger to subjectivity, this is because – limited as it is to its experience as subject and unable to recognize the process that leads to the constant transmutation of itself and the world – it simply has no way of holding itself up through this process. Precluded from imagining another world and from imagining itself differently from what it considers to be itself, subjectivity protects itself by believing that "the world," its world, can last forever, just the way it is.

Paralyzed by the fear caused by the imaginary risk of a breakdown, subjectivity is overwhelmed by specters that haunt it. These image-beings are projected onto subjectivity's experiences, and this keeps subjectivity dissociated from its own experiences. The specters that haunt it cause subjectivity to erroneously interpret the malaise brought about by destabilization as if it were a "bad thing." This sense of malaise (a vital emotion) thus gets turned into anguish (a psychological feeling).

Unlike the micropolitics corresponding to the opposite pole we described above (the active pole), what we're dealing with here is a subjectivity that can support itself neither in the tension of the paradox of its experiences as both subject and as outside-the-subject nor in the paradoxical movements that its friction unleashes, the same movements that constitute the drive-unconscious. In this case, the cuts made by desire will seek to avoid the question mark that the vibration of the seed of a world nestled in subjectivity raises for that same subjectivity. Desire is called upon to quickly bring back an equilibrium; it seeks equilibrium guided by a moral compass, whose needle points to a cartography where life finds itself materialized in the topological-relational surface of the world in its present form. The moral needle leads desire towards modes of existence and representations produced in previous cuts. Desire then chooses one of those modes to go on cutting, and, in so doing, it allows subjectivity to quickly remake for itself a recognizable outline that brings relief to it: relief from its anguish; temporary relief. And so the world becomes a vast and varied marketplace where subjectivity has at its disposal countless images to identify with and with which to establish a relationship of consumption that will allow it to recover the fleeting respite of an imaginary balance. Desire's choice of cut in this opulent marketplace depends on each subjectivity's repertoire and on how subjectivity interprets the reason behind its discomfort.

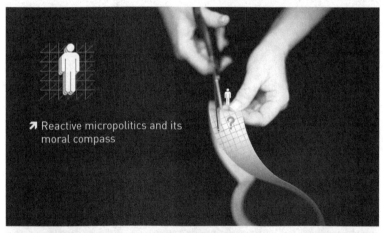

↗ Reactive micropolitics and its moral compass

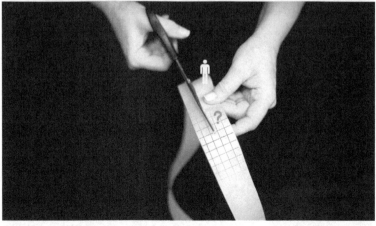

34 Colonial-Capitalistic Unconscious

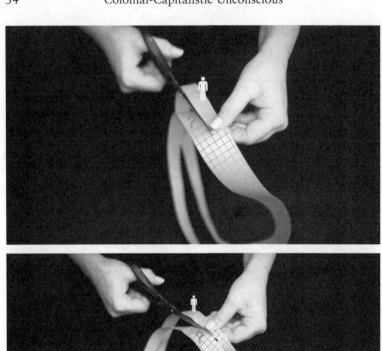
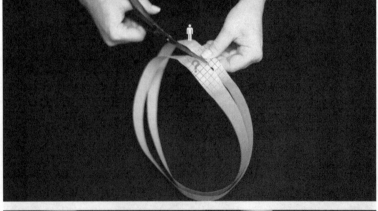

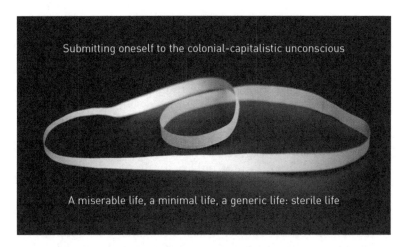

Because unease is interpreted as a "bad thing," someone, of course, must bear the blame. Reduced to the subject, subjectivity has only two ways to determine who is to be blamed for its state of instability, both options being the result of phantasmatic constructions: either the subject itself or someone else is chosen to play the role of villain. In other words, subjectivity either introjects the cause of its destabilization as a supposed deficiency of itself (which suffuses its anguish with feelings of guilt, inferiority, and shame), or subjectivity projects the cause of this destabilization onto an imagined evil masterminded from the outside (which suffuses its anguish with paranoid feelings, with hate, and with resentment).

When Self-Deprecation, Guilt, and Shame Interrupt the Germination of a World

In the first of these cases (introjection), in an attempt to placate the feeling of self-deprecation and shame, desire will choose the point in the topological-relational surface of the world that is most clearly adequate for the purpose of appeasement. That's where psychiatric prescription drugs enter the picture. Their market feeds precisely from the dismay herein described, contributing to its perpetuation. This is because, in pathologizing the experience of destabilization, the prescription of these medications confirms

36 Colonial-Capitalistic Unconscious

both the phantasmatic interpretation of the underlying cause of instability and the anguish that it provokes.[18] Subjectivity uses prescription drugs to try and neutralize its anguish.

The fact that its anguish is chemically controlled does not at all imply that subjectivity will be more willing to feel what is signaled to it by its eco-ethological knowledge (which isn't to say that the use of certain chemical substances couldn't enhance this same sensibility). The point is that these medications, when prescribed for such purposes without accounting for the affects that caused the anguish, not only neutralize anguish; they also neutralize the affects that caused anguish, without necessarily facilitating the recomposition of the subject's previous outline. Even though these medications do not offer to it the response it had hoped for, the subject insists on regaining its equilibrium at all costs, remaining in the same place. Because of this, other points, just as known, will be chosen by desire to make its cuts.

To give some sense to the nonsensical state where subjectivity finds itself, desire can also connect with products offered by discourse dealers peddling recipes for a redeeming peace, *and with these products it can make its cuts on the relational topological surface of the world.* The supply is abundant: self-esteem training therapies; self-help books and books announcing a so-called *new age*; ideologies of every sort; evangelical churches of the fundamentalist type[19] (which have proliferated to the point where you can find them in every corner of the planet). Also available for consumption are Eastern religions, emptied of their original sense.

As a matter of fact, those Eastern religions do have the potential to lead subjectivity to experiences that (re)conquer body-knowing, the kind of knowing proper to living beings. This is because they attribute this knowing to terrestrial beings and not to a supposed god, and they cultivate the development of this knowing from the moment of birth up to the moment of death, in both individual and collective rituals. This makes them more of a philosophy or an ethics of existence than a religion, in the sense that Westerners tend to conceive of and practice religion. Nonetheless, when these philosophies are practiced by subjectivities reduced to subjects, they tend to transform them into religions in the Western sense. The mindfulness furnished by Eastern meditation (which would lead subjectivity to connect with the knowledge proper to living beings) is reduced to an emptying of the mind of the subject: a clearing of its threatening ghosts, in a way that reduces the subject's anguish. A supposed truth (arising from imaginary and esoteric forces) takes the place of what would emerge from the connection with the knowledge proper to living beings. The rituals, which should work as ways of appropriating this kind of knowing, are instead turned into nurseries that coddle needy, helpless, white Western people, providing them with the self-image of "evolved" and "spiritualized" beings. This image calms them down for a bit, allowing them to stay in the same place, *as if nothing were happening, as if there were no turbulences making their position untenable.* All these recipes for the attainment of "peace" bring about ghostly hallucinations, which are then projected onto reality and superimposed onto its decoding. These projected hallucinations come hand in hand with actions that allow the subject to channel the energy of its anguish, bringing an illusion of control back to it.

In that same register, desire will also be able to connect subjectivity to complex intellectual discourses that will also be put to hallucinatory use, reducing these discourses to skeletons of dry and empty rhetoric, barren of flesh (the flesh of a living body). In short, when the subject establishes this type of relationship to theoretical discourses, their potency to affect that same subject is neutralized, nullifying the resonance that these affects could have had on it. Hindering this resonance dissolves its power either to promote the subject's reappropriation of body-knowing or to expand this knowing, if its exercise is already underway. It doesn't really matter at which discursive point desire chooses to make its cut: "low culture," or sophisticated philosophical cartwheels, or anything in between. The fact is that, from the perspective of the politics of desire I'm describing here, different visions of the world are rendered equivalent, because the relationship that subjectivity establishes with any one of them is the same. It is a relationship of consumption that seeks to temporarily recover a voice by means of its mere echo. Regardless of which vision is adopted in this process, it gets used as a clichéd discourse, a guide for a subjectivity that, dissociated from its condition as living being, cannot be in tune with what is happening to it, much less find the words to express it. To fill this void, subjectivity consumes words foreign to it and wrapped in an aura of truth, which allows subjectivity to idealize these words and to rid itself of self-deprecation through the act of mouthing these same words. This is what makes subjectivity such an easy target for any image or discourse, and this is what makes it adopt clichéd discourses as if they were its core beliefs.

But chemicals and discursive platforms alone do not guarantee the composition of an outline that can bring balance back to subjectivity. In order to free itself from the shame and the fear of exclusion that its own self-deprecation causes, subjectivity will also have to mimic lifestyles that bring back to it a feeling of belonging. This is a condition necessary for this kind of subjectivity (separated from its out-of-subject experience) to feel itself existing. To do that, desire will connect to products that the market offers for every taste and for every social segment, products seductively peddled by mass and social media. These products are always presented couched in images of certain fantasy worlds, characterized by idyllic scenarios, and starring idealized characters. Dazzled, subjectivity will try to mimic these characters through the consumption of products associated with such scenarios: suppliers of ready-to-wear performances for its false self (this is even more evident in the case of advertising). Like psychiatric pharmaceutical products, like churches, like so-called spiritual practices, ideologies, self-esteem stimulators, and complex intellectual discourses, these consumer goods are used as perfumes to mask the infectious stench of a stagnant life.

When Hate and Resentment Interrupt the Germination of a New World

In the second case described above, where the cause of the malaise is interpreted by subjectivity as an evil masterminded from the outside, desire will choose as its cutting point something that works as a scapegoat. This will be a body that subjectivity can empty from its singularity so that it can transform it into a blank canvas onto which it can project the reason for its malaise, which is then converted into hate and resentment. The demonized other can be a person, a people, a skin color, a social class, a type of sexuality, an ideology, a political party, a state leader, etc. This is what xenophobias amount to, what Islamophobias, homophobias, transphobias, and so many other phobias really are, and this, too, is what racisms, antisemitisms, machismos, chauvinisms, nationalisms, and other -isms constitute. They can

Colonial-Capitalistic Unconscious

lead to extremely violent actions, whose power of contagion tends to create the conditions necessary for the rise of a fascist mass.

We have more than enough examples of this phenomenon in our current day and age. In the case of Brazil, suffice it to cite a phenomenon that took place during the media campaign that set the stage for the most recent coup d'état. Street protests gathered thousands of people, many of them wearing the Brazilian flag and calling fervently for the impeachment of President Dilma Rousseff. Some, many of them, went as far as requesting the return of the military dictatorship to Brazil.

Regardless of which cutting points were chosen in either case of phantasmatic interpretation – introjection or projection – of the cause of the malaise brought about by destabilization, the actions of desire governed by a reactive micropolitics result in a decrease of the potency of our condition as living beings. This produces a kind of vital anemia, no less powerful in its effects. Like those cuts in the Möbius strip (in *Caminhando*) made against the instructions provided by Lygia Clark, what results from the reactive politics of desire is the eternal reproduction of forms of the world in its present configuration.

Under the impact of a reactive micropolitics ruled by a moral compass, subjectivity dissociates itself even further from what happens to it. And, if we expand the horizon of our gaze to include the topological-relational surface of the world as it is currently configured, we will verify that what grows weaker is precisely the collective potency for creation and cooperation, which is necessary for the construction of the common, which emanates from the power to rise in revolt, and which at the same time strengthens this power. On the contrary, what gets promoted is the conservation of the status quo. This is the micropolitics of an existence, individual or collective, that allows its vital, creating potency to be expropriated and that gives itself away voluntarily, in some cases even fervently.

In short, when we compare the active and reactive politics of the actions of desire, we see that the first case effectively brings about a new equilibrium by means of an act of creation that transmutes reality with its instituting force. In the second case, in the case of reactive politics, equilibrium is regained fictitiously and fleetingly by an act that interrupts the destiny of the potency of creation of life, reducing this potency to "creativity." Because

40   Colonial-Capitalistic Unconscious

creativity is only one of the abilities essential for the work of creation, when it is dissociated from body-knowing it becomes sterile, and it does nothing beyond merely recomposing what is already instituted. Here, desire stops acting in sync with what life demands from it, and it turns away from its ethical function.

There lies the poison of the micropolitics immanent to modern, Western, colonial-capitalistic culture. Its toxic effects consist in the separation of subjectivity from its germinating drive-force and the after-effects of this separation: the desirous potency of creation of worlds that would dissolve the elements of the cartography of the present (where life finds itself asphyxiated) becomes stagnant. Dissociated in such a way, subjectivity is ready to allow this potency to be pimped out by capital. Desire's actions will be guided in that direction, building conditions so that the drive finds jouissance in being pimped.

Ruled by that type of micropolitics, desire starts to function as a reactive agent that interrupts the process of creating worlds. Given that the seeds of new worlds that live inside all bodies emerge from the encounters between different bodies (thus forming the field that encompasses all of them and turns them into one single body), disrupting the germination of these seeds in someone's life also causes, indissociably, a point of putre-faction in the life of its environment. In other words, each life that does not rise to the challenge of what happens to it spoils the life of its whole relational web. The poison produced by this kind of life propagates across its relational threads like a plague, poisoning them and stagnating their continuous process of differ-entiation. These are the effects of a life subjected to the perverse power of the colonial-capitalistic unconscious. A generic life, a minimal life, a sterile life: a miserable life.

When Perverse Abuse Refines Itself

As we have seen, in the context of financialized, globalitarian capitalism, the perverse abuse of the force of labor (in the expansive sense of the term, which includes every type of "work" performed by the vital force) is transmuted, fine-tuned, and intensified. This abuse, as we already noted, constitutes the essence of the colonial-capitalistic mode of operation. We're now far removed from the identity regime that structured subjectivity

Colonial-Capitalistic Unconscious 41

under Fordism and that gave it the form of its labor force (in the literal sense of the term "labor force") and of its cooperation. A flexible subjectivity is produced in this new fold, one that now manages its own drive-potency, which, as mentioned earlier, gives subjectivity the impression that it is free to decide the destiny of this potency.

However, because subjectivity is reduced to the subject, desire tends to divert this potency away from its ethical destiny, in hopes of guaranteeing the subject's supposed stability and in hopes of holding up its sense of belonging. What emerges from this process are forms of existence where the drive-potency is available for its free extraction, for the accumulation of economic, political, and cultural capital. It is therefore by means of the actions of desire that subjectivity will feed the accumulation of capital and its power, offering itself gleefully to this "sacrifice" – like the sex worker who, under the pimp's seductive spell, offers herself to him in hopes of securing from him not just a means of survival but the very right to exist.

This alone would be enough to foster the production of reactive desire. But there are other factors that converge so that this becomes the predominant destiny of the drive-potency, which is now believed to be self-managed. With the advances in technologies of information and communication, which come faster and faster in the current regime, the malaise brought about by paradox (which is the propelling engine of processes of subjectivation) becomes more frequent and more intense. Flexible subjectivity is constantly bombarded by images of worlds and by narratives, and this process is aggravated by the automated proliferation of these images and these narratives, which multiplies them ad infinitum. This, in turn, renders the subject's already ephemeral contours ever more rapidly obsolete, which intensifies its fragility.

Confronted with this, and because it is reduced to the subject, subjectivity becomes more vulnerable to the imposition of ready-to-wear responses, which, as already noted, are offered in abundance by those same technological and communication platforms. That dynamic creates the grounds to support essential aspects of the new regime. The economic advantages of this dynamic are obvious: consumer goods find in this worsened fragility the basis of their guaranteed demand, which in turn allows for their infinite multiplication. This dynamic is reinforced

42   Colonial-Capitalistic Unconscious

by the subject's phantasmatic interpretation of its own fragility: it reads its fragility as a threat of exclusion (exclusion by self-deprecation or by a paranoid sense of persecution). If under industrial capitalism this threat made subjectivity more vulnerable to the spell of images that the market offered to it, in the new fold of the regime this vulnerability tends to get exacerbated. The reason is that the subject's phantasmatic interpretation of its own fragility also gets exploited in the power strategy introduced by this new fold, where micropolitical procedures join the more traditional macropolitical procedures. In some countries (Brazil, for instance), these macropolitical procedures emerge from a triple alliance composed by the judicial and legislative powers and by the power of the media.

When Power Uses Desire as its Principal Weapon

If mass media has constituted an important piece of equipment for the exercise of power since industrial capitalism, under the new version of the regime this equipment gains unprecedented prominence, largely due to technological advances that allow for generalized communications in real time. A case in point: the series of strategies (described below) that have been implemented in several South American countries since the early years of the twenty-first century.

Let's take Brazil as an example. Using cherry-picked and edited information gathered and chosen by an alliance between the judiciary and the police, the mass media has come up with narratives broadcast in dramatic tones, narratives that amplify and aggravate an image of economic crisis (the transnational nature of which is actively obscured) and of the danger this crisis is supposed to bring with it. This sends subjectivity running for the proverbial hills, in search of exits conveniently constructed by the same media narratives, using the fictitious figure of a scapegoat that bears responsibility for the crisis, which is also fictitiously construed. Figures or parties targeted for expulsion from the political stage will be the first to be cast in the role of the scapegoat, conceived in the process of information cherry-picking mentioned above.

Broadcast day in day and day out, repeated often and in various dramatic tones, these narratives offer a plethora of signals that confirm a feared scenario fabulated by a subjectivity reduced to the subject: a scenario that includes the imagined threat of imminent disaggregation. As it gives in to that fear (to a point that surpasses the limits of what can be metabolized, to a point where fear becomes traumatic), subjectivity latches onto the story of the scapegoat and projects on it the cause of its malaise, as if this were its only way out, or the closest exit available. This is the reason why these narratives are met with relief and embraced as truths. They justify the malaise experienced by these subjectivities and provide them with conditions to expel it, projecting it onto the other. Moreover, the fact that so many are prone to adopt these highly viral narratives generates a feeling of belonging in subjectivities that (given their lack of access to the living body of the world to which they belong) feel isolated and fear being humiliated and excluded from social coexistence. Massive public protests attended by that kind of subjectivity constitute a collective ritual that offers to its participants the sensation of belonging to a homogenous community, one that forms a presumably stable whole and that can substitute the multiple and variable construction of the common, protecting subjectivities from the imaginary threat that this construction constitutes for them.

Based on that induced trauma, conditions are provided for the unlimited power of globalitarian capitalism, which involves taking over state power in contexts where this power is not already entirely in the hands of transnational capitalism. This is achieved by means of certain operations that alternate and come together and that are practiced with varying degrees of intensity. The first such operation are elections disguised as expressions of popular will – a will that, in fact, is nothing more than the result of populist manipulation performed through the procedures outlined above. The second such operation consists in election fraud, and the third is the impeachment of elected officials on the grounds of apparently justified legal reasons, whenever necessary.

This kind of impeachment process (like the one orchestrated against President Dilma Rousseff in Brazil) is brought about by legislative bodies who appeal to juridical fictions to camouflage impeachment as an effort to restore democracy. These fictions give impeachment the sheen of legitimacy, and they mobilize broad popular support (legitimacy and support that, in this case, are manufactured by the dissemination of juridical fictions in social and mass media). If coups d'état previously conducted by military forces served the interests of industrial capitalism, the coup d'état as intervention is no longer useful for financialized capitalism. Totalitarian states are a thorn in the side of the free circulation of capital. Furthermore, these kinds of states promote identitarian principles, whereas the new regime requires flexible subjectivities.

Instead of military force, globalitarian capitalism uses two kinds of weapons: a micropolitical weapon (the drive-potency and its emissary, desire) and a macropolitical weapon (an alliance with the most reactive local political forces). The two weapons are grafted onto each other. These reactive local political forces are embodied in ignorant, crude, brutish, and extremely conservative characters: remnants of a pre-financialized capitalism and also, to boot, of an archaic, pre-republican, colonial, and slavocrat mentality that never stopped being the dominant one in Brazil.[20] These pathetic characters are used as straw men, and they do the dirty work of expelling progressive local politicians off the stage, preparing the ground for the rise to power of financialized capitalism, transnational by its very nature.

In Brazil, it's easy to find these kinds of figures in the legislative, the executive, and the judicial branches of government, where they've always been, changing nothing other than their discourse and procedures. To cite but two of the more obvious examples, let us consider the case of rural representatives in the Brazilian National Congress, stakeholders in the same agrobusiness that devastates ecosystems and either expels indigenous communities from their ancestral lands – lands reclaimed in the 1988 Constitution – or literally decimates them in a genocide that goes unpunished and that doesn't even register in local media. The second example of these kinds of figures consist of evangelical representatives (or at least their vast majority), with their hypocritical moralism and their staunch, heteronormative, patriarchal, and "family values" sexism, which falsely derives legitimacy from supposedly divine will.

More widely speaking, we can find these figures embodied in corrupt government officials and politicians who proliferate indistinctly across all party lines and who provide, in exchange for bribes from private companies, conditions favorable for spurious business deals with the state, through a process of corrupt enrichment made possible by overbilling and other such ruses. The most obvious example of companies that engage in this kind of business are construction companies hired to build public works. These are "local" companies that are nonetheless flush with transnational capital (a few conglomerates, such as Odebrecht in Brazil, are exceptions to this way of doing business).

The dirty work performed by reactive, local, political forces consists in, first and foremost, the preparation and the execution of plans for the expulsion of progressive politicians from the stage. Once this first task is completed, the second task consists in the implementation of measures that must be taken quickly by the executive branch and/or the legislative branch of government, measures that are often approved in the dead of the night, when everyone is sleeping, or during congressional recesses (especially Christmas and New Year's Eve, when everyone is distracted with compulsive shopping and family celebrations, gripped as everyone is by the anxious desire to stage an image of happiness and harmony). The delirious rhythm of these measures is hard to follow, and by the time society, or at least part of it, becomes aware of one of these measures, another one, just as violent, has already been approved, and once again it goes unnoticed. It goes without saying that these measures basically consist in the dismantling of workers' rights and of safety net programs; in the absolution of the state's responsibilities in the education, health, housing, and urban planning sectors, with particularly pernicious consequences for the most vulnerable segments of the population; and in the privatization of the maximum amount of public goods, especially those goods coveted by private capital given their high degree of profitability.

Once the dirty work is done, a second chapter begins, wherein the characters who did this dirty work are themselves ejected, through the same juridical-mediatic procedures that drove progressive politicians off the stage. The strategy consists in producing, day in and day out, arrest warrants for such politicians and for the high-ranking executives linked to them. Plea bargains (curiously known in Brazil as *delações premiadas*, "rewarded snitching") are used to force these characters into accusing each other, which yields information linked to the corruption of other politicians (politicians belonging to the same parties of those who served as straw men in the overthrow of progressive administrations). These corrupt politicians become the new main characters, and they now get to play the role of scapegoats in the narrative peddled by the media. This, however, does not mean that politicians affiliated to progressive political parties are off the hook; they only stop being targets when they're finally destroyed.

Two problems get solved thanks to the operations outlined above. First, pathetic characters are purged through both prosecution and the consequent termination of their right to serve in public office. This brings the added benefit of giving the operation an air of impartiality, to the extent that it makes it seem as if it were politically neutral, because it targets not just leftist political parties but other parties as well, which in turn props up the belief that the elimination of corruption is the true focus here and that this has nothing to do with political affiliations. More credibility is thus generated for the false constitutional legitimacy surrounding the coup d'état – a coup which, moreover, is extended by virtue of that whole operation, because it keeps going well after the impeachment is over. The ground is thus cleared for the rise to power of administrators proficient in the latest version of capitalism, who will pave the way for a more efficient traffic of financialized capital into and out of the space of the national, obliterating any obstacle that stands in the way of its free circulation.

The second problem solved through the operations outlined above is exemplified in Brazil but not limited to it. It has to do with local businessmen (especially from the public works construction and the agrobusiness sectors) imprisoned on charges of corruption and thus purged from the economic stage. These are businessmen who made inroads in markets beyond Brazil (mainly in Latin American and Africa), the majority of which were conquered by administrations led by the PT (Partido dos Trabalhadores, the Workers' Party in Brazil). More opportunities for highly profitable businesses are thus made available to transnational capital. And all this is welcomed with open arms by a large swath of the Brazilian population who now completely identify with the media narrative.

The last chapter of that story will surely consist in the unveiling of financialized capital in the role of national hero, a savior that, if granted complete control of the country, will give back dignity to national public life, restoring the national economy after the severe economic crisis deliberately orchestrated in the preceding chapters. In Latin America, these proceedings are used to dismantle progressive governments established in the last few decades in some of the nations of the region after the dissolution of their respective military dictatorships, which took place throughout the 1980s. The moment the left rises to power is also the moment when the new modality of the coup d'état begins to take shape, in a process witnessed by society as it were watching a TV series. The first testing ground for this new strategy of power was the removal of Fernando Lugo as president of Paraguay in 2012.[21]

Once the efficacy of the new modality of the coup had been tried and tested in Paraguay, the production of the series in Brazil (which was first conceived in 2002 after Lula was elected president) accelerated and grew in intensity with each passing day, the series "apparently" culminating in the impeachment of President Dilma Rousseff in 2016 ("apparently" because the new modality of the coup does not stop with the removal of the president). In the mass demonstrations organized to call for her removal from office, the mantra "Dilma is to blame" slowly and uncontrollably took hold in plazas and streets all over Brazil. This mantra arose precisely from the fiction the media had constructed for wide public consumption, a fiction which featured President Dilma, the Brazilian Workers' Party, and the members of this party (especially its leader, Lula da Silva) as principal characters – that is to say, as scapegoats.[22]

The same series has also started to play out in other Latin American countries in places where progressive officials elected to office have not yet completed their terms. In other cases, where elected officials have almost finished their term, the mediatic-juridical-parliamentary strategy inscribes itself in the preparations leading up to elections in a way that prevents the most progressive candidates from even running for office. This, in turn, reduces races to a contest between neoliberal candidates and ultraconservative ones. As we saw above, these ultraconservative candidates are nothing but an undesirable, collateral effect of their empowerment by financialized capitalism, which relies on them to prepare its rise to power. This is what happened in Peru[23] in a recent presidential race where, in the first round of the election, the progressive candidate lost by a wide margin to the neoliberal candidate.

48 Colonial-Capitalistic Unconscious

The latter went on to win the runoff by a narrow margin, against an ultraconservative.

Abuse Produces Traumas and Feeds on Them

The flexible subjectivity produced by this regime is therefore, and as a matter of principle, constantly kept in a state of fragility bordering on trauma. Often, this state of fragility goes past the threshold of trauma, sinking subjectivity into a breakdown. This is achieved by means of the three procedures outlined above: the reduction of subjectivity to the subject; the constant collapse of its forms of existence and of its respective meanings; and the masking of this collapse through an immediate supply of fictitious narratives instilled daily on subjectivity by the media.

There is, furthermore, a fourth procedure deployed by financialized capitalism that contributes to the weakening of subjectivity, especially among the most disenfranchised segments of the population. It revolves around the figure of the "gig worker" (poorly paid, unprotected, and insecure) resulting from the deregulation of labor and the consequent deterioration of work conditions, legalized by the nullification of workers' rights by neoliberal states. This figure is legitimized by the fiction that, under this scheme, workers gain autonomy to negotiate the value of their work as well as their rights. This illusion is sustained by the destruction of the progressive imaginary outlined above, and, at the same time, it feeds into and reinforces the same destruction of this imaginary.

This deregulation of labor, combined with the supposed autonomy it brings to workers, leaves subjectivities more traumatized and unable to act. And this is when they become more vulnerable to abuse, ready to make their drive-force available for pimping, duped by the illusion that being pimped out will somehow bring back their outline, along with a sense of place. More generally speaking, this is also how the collective potency of creation and cooperation is channeled towards the maintenance and the nourishment of the status quo: either through the appropriation of the labor force, through unhinged consumption, through mass support for coups d'état or for electoral fraud, or through other micropolitical strategies of the regime not mentioned here. In short, this is how the potency of desire is deviated from its ethical destiny – which is to say, from its active and creating performance – so that capital can appropriate it and transform it into a reactive potency of submission.

This is where the perversion of the colonial-capitalistic regime in its new version resides, and this, too, is where its real danger lies. The regime feeds on the imaginary threat generated in subjectivity by its separation from its condition as living being. At the same time, it feeds the phantom of that threat, thus keeping subjectivity captive in its reduction. The situation we are now experiencing is an incubator for that very real danger, and there is no guarantee that this danger can be averted. The use of micropolitical strategies by financialized transnational capitalism in its efforts to seize macropolitical power – combined with its use of politicians to do its dirty work and with conservatism on the rise – has a great chance of producing a crisis of unmanageable proportions.

This is exactly what is already taking place, what poisons the atmosphere and makes it unbreathable. Trump's election to the presidency of the United States and the election of far-right candidates in Europe, along with Brexit and the glimpse of a dismantled European Union, are only the most glaring symptoms. There is no lack of examples at the local level in Brazil; they are so numerous that listing them would take up an infinite amount of space, sidetracking us from our focus. Besides, listing these examples would be unnecessary and redundant. They have been thoroughly covered in everyday news, and there is a vast bibliography that describes them and analyzes them. What matters is that we recognize the following: in the unstable balance and temporary association between neoliberalism and extreme conservatism, the scales can very well tip towards the latter, and with full support of the masses. Like a well-organized group of sports fans, these masses regress towards the identitarian principle in its maximum degree of rigidness – at the individual level, at the group level (class, ethnicity, gender, race, etc.), and at the national level. Today, this threat looms over our planet, and for transnational capital this means, in principle, a threat of obstruction for its free flow.

We see, then, that financialized capital's gamble seems to be backfiring. This does not bring us any advantage, because, albeit in different ways, both scenarios are just as nefarious: the pimp-colonial-capitalistic regime in its new version, on the one

50 Colonial-Capitalistic Unconscious

hand, or the return of a nationalist conservatism, archaic and lethal (an inevitable effect of the regime itself, which through its own logic leads to its crisis), on the other. It is not a matter of choosing the lesser evil. Intrinsically linked as they are, what is worse is precisely their explosive combination. The word "sinister" at the beginning of this essay refers to that situation; it describes our current atmosphere with precision. The mix of different periods in the history of capitalism, all of them at their most perverse, adds even more complexity to the dynamics of power and, consequently, to their deciphering and to the invention of strategies to confront them.

If this is an alarming picture, we must recognize that, because it is so, it leads those of us confronting it to realize that we need to expand and add complexity to our notion of resistance and, more widely speaking, to the very notion of politics. This generates a sense of encouraging relief, against the tendency to give into fear, and against the habitual reactions that fear provokes: melancholic paralysis, or a haste to act quickly to get rid of fear, holding tight to old conceptions of resistance that no longer make sense. This may well be the case with the very concept of resistance, marked as it is by a logic of negation, of opposition, of non-acceptance: marked, in other words, by a reactive tendency, which does not include the positivity of an active transforming action.

Faced with this new scenario, it is clearly not enough to assume responsibility as a citizen and to fight for a more equitable distribution of material and immaterial goods, of civil rights and, more widely and fundamentally, of the very right to exist. This is the bare minimum that we must long for, and when we cannot manage to assume even this responsibility, it is because dissociation has reached an alarming degree of pathology. But, beyond that task, it is also necessary to take on the responsibility we have as living beings and to fight for the reappropriation of the potencies of creation and cooperation and for the construction of the common that depends on this reappropriation. In other words, it is not enough to fight in the sphere of macropolitical power against those who hold this power. We must also fight for the affirming potency of an active micropolitics, to be invested in every one of our everyday activities, including those that involve our relationship to the state, regardless of whether we move within it or outside it. Isn't

Colonial-Capitalistic Unconscious   *51*

this precisely the fight put up by the new type of activism now proliferating all over the planet?

It is thus indispensable to think and act in the direction of an active micropolitics in such a way that we can confront the situation on different levels and simultaneously: at the level of subjectivity, of desire, and of thought. This is the sphere where financialized, transnational capitalism supports itself existentially, both in its neoliberal and in its conservative facet (conservatism being the monstrous and self-generated adversary of the regime). Waging this battle depends on our capacity to break the spell of tsunamic power cast by the reactive micropolitics of globalitarian capitalism which spreads over every sphere of human life, destroying its modes of life and, above all, destroying life's essential potency of creation and transmutation.

All this implies dis-identifying with the modes of existence constructed by the regime to substitute those it devastates, so we can abandon those ways of living. This must be done not in order to return to past modes of existence but in order to invent different ones, as a function of the seeds of the future incubating in the present. Only in this way does the idea of reappropriating the collective force of creation and cooperation – the indisputable means to confront the current state of things – have any chance of being more than words on a page, more than utopian dreams. Only then does this idea have a chance of becoming reality.

When Thinking and Resisting Become One and the Same Thing

I argued towards the beginning of this essay that neither a decree of the will nor the good intentions of consciousness will allow us to act towards the reappropriation of the collective force of creation and cooperation. Perhaps now it is easier to understand why I emphasized that this is a task that each one of us must perform, on our own subjectivity and on the relational plot inextricably linked to it, and in a way that allows us to break free from our submission to the power of the colonial-capitalistic unconscious. Perhaps now it is also easier to understand why I insisted that there's a need, inseparable from this work, to break free in the realm of thinking, not just in relation to the content of thought but in relation to the principle that governs

52 Colonial-Capitalistic Unconscious

its production and guides its contents, as well as its ways of evaluating the present.

If we consider the fact that each mode of production of subjectivity and desire corresponds to a mode of production of thought, it can be helpful to return to the two fictitious poles (the most active and the most reactive) in the expansive range of possible micropolitics, so we can briefly examine the distinction between the principles that govern the production of thought in each one of these micropolitics, and the different effects these principles have on the destinies of social life.

Considered from its ethical perspective, which governs the actions of desire on the active end of the spectrum, thinking means "listening" to affects: to the larval worlds generated in the body by the forces that constitute the environment. It means "getting involved" in the deterritorializing movement triggered by these larval worlds. Lastly, guided by these acts of listening and getting-involved-with, thinking also means to "create" an expression for *what demands to come through*, an expression that can give *this* a concrete body. When practiced from that perspective, the effects of thinking are usually as follows: a "potentializing contagion" of subjectivities that are in contact with it – or, more precisely, a "pollination"[24] of these subjectivities; the "transfiguration" of the topological-relational surface of a world in its present form (brought about by the irruption of that strange body on its familiar outline); and the "transvaluation" of the values that predominate in it.

On the other hand, from the perspective of the reactive end of the spectrum, thinking means "becoming numb" to affects, to the turbulences caused by affects, and to the demands of life necessarily mobilized by affects. It means "reflecting," like a mirror, an alleged truth presumed to be hiding in the darkness of ignorance, one that would supposedly "explain" the deterritorializing movement (this alleged truth is the delirium that covers the very cause of deterritorialization and pretends to solve it, interrupting its movement). Thinking, from this perspective, also means "revealing" that alleged truth, "enlightening it" with the searchlight of reason – in this case, a reason restricted to empty rhetorical formulas whose origins lie in the dissociation from real experience. In sum, thinking in the sense I have in mind here means rationalizing the discomfort. It means denying what estranges us by transforming it into what is familiar. The effect of thinking as practiced from this perspective tends to be the "de-potentializing contagion" of subjectivities that are in contact with whoever exercises this form of thinking, which contributes to the "interruption of the process of pollination" and thus promotes an "abortion of the germination of futures." What results from that is the "reproduction" of the present cartography and its values.

I use the term "anthropo-phallo-ego-logocentric" to describe the reactive politics of the production of thought outlined above, which is governed by the colonial-capitalistic unconscious regime. Confronted with its power, which spreads more and more every day, it is not enough to problematize the concepts that this politics has produced and continues to produce; we must problematize the very principle that governs it. This challenge implies activating in us the knowing that comes from being alive, and to do so in the very exercise of thought in such a way that it releases thought from its prison of dry logocentrism and from its false problems – all consequences of its divorce from life and from the real problems that its movements bring to thought. We must stay on the lookout for that which body-knowing points out for us. This attitude is the basis of the force and the astuteness necessary to resist the power of the gang of phantasms born out of the submission to the colonial-capitalistic unconsciousness (which governs subjectivities and orients the movements of desire). It makes sense, then, to say that thinking and insurrecting are one and the same thing.

But What Does Art Have to Do with All of This?

Undeniably, artistic practices have a lot to teach us as we face the need to resist in the realm of the production of thought and of its actions. What art shows us is the possibility of replacing the anthropo-phallo-ego-logocentric perspective with an ethical-aesthetic-clinical-political one. It also shows us a way to undertake this crossover.

We cannot deny that the potency of art has been weakened under the current regime. In Western and Westernized societies, where art as an institution originated just over two centuries ago, art was until recently the only field of human activity that authorized exercising the potency of creation, which made

54   Colonial-Capitalistic Unconscious

sensible the virtual worlds pulsing in the bodies fertilized by the spirit of their times. Until recently, the actualization of these worlds could take place only in so-called works of art – paintings, sculptures, installations, and so forth. But when these works embodied the pulse of worlds to come, they had the power to pollinate the environments where these works circulated, beyond the field of art.

Moreover, and not coincidentally, under the new version of the pimp-colonial-capitalistic regime, art became a specially coveted field, a privileged source of appropriation of the creating force by capital for the purpose of instrumentalizing this force. This opened a new frontier for the accumulation of capital, as art makes possible one of the fastest and most extraordinary multiplications of investment capital. Among the reasons behind this, it bears mentioning two of them. The buying power of new international elites offers them the possibility of participating in museum boards and thus of rubbing shoulders with the cream of the crop of museum patrons. In return, this allows them to choose those artists who will have their works collected and/or exhibited by those museums, thus increasing their market value and exponentially multiplying the capital they have invested in these artists' works. Art investments, of course, are among the most successful vehicles for money laundering.

But art instrumentalization by this regime doesn't stop there. Its objectives are not strictly macropolitical (conquering political power through the accumulation of economic power); its objectives are also micropolitical, and there are many such objectives in this sphere. The first one consists in neutralizing the transfiguring force of artistic practices, reducing them to mere exercises of creativity and dissociating this force from its ethical function: the creation of a body that can express what life announces. The second micropolitical objective consists in using art as a passport to the international salons organized by the elites of financialized capitalism.

The reason behind this second objective is evident. The look necessary for admission into such salons depends on a certain lifestyle: being an art collector; having two or three names rolling off one's tongue (the names of artists and curators, of the latest darlings of the art world, the ones who, not coincidentally, are on the crest of the tidal wave of the art market); traveling around the world as tourists in the global circuit of institutional spaces consecrated to art (especially the most prestigious ones). To be a consumer of contemporary art, or at the very least to be seen parading around its halls, differentiates these elites from those other traditional elites of capitalism before its financialization. For the more recent elites, this is a way of staving off the risk of being perceived as tacky, as tasteless, a perception that can stymie their businesses. This is all especially pathetic in the case of South American elites (and in the case of other elites from former European colonies) who, when donning this look, reveal the ridiculous false self they need to mask their evidently low self-esteem.

This dynamic, of course, has an impact on artistic production. The fact that these new international elites dominate the art market with their buying power tends to lead artists to mold themselves according to demands imposed on them as a condition to enter the halls of the elite, as if they were luxury goods. This is how the potency of creation is also redirected in this field, away from its ethical destiny and in the service of producing commodity artworks.

Because all of this is now widely known, to describe it here in exhaustive detail would be a waste of time. It's worth noting, however, that, precisely due to the increasing difficulty of practicing thought from an ethical-aesthetic-clinical-political perspective even in the field of art, many artists have dedicated themselves to projects that make the problematization of this state of affairs (in the art field and beyond it) the raw material of their work. As discussed towards the beginning of this essay, these practices tend to go beyond the boundaries of art. They're housed in a transterritoriality where all manner of activist practices are also housed – feminist activism, environmental activism, antiracist activism, indigenous activism, LGBTQI activism, housing justice activism, antigentrification activism, and so forth. The encounters and misencounters between these different practices produce singular becomings of each of these practices, in the direction of the construction of a common.

And here I pose a question for us, dear reader: Where does the political potency of art reside, if not in the event of those becomings? This is very different from a certain idea of "political art" or "socially engaged art," the kind that turns art practices into pamphlets, into macropolitical vehicles of awareness, denunciation, and ideological transmission. Rather, what's at stake in this question is a micropolitical potency intrinsic to art. It has been asserting itself in some artistic practices in successive cycles since the 1960s, cycles where those practices come together to exert this same aesthetic-political potency in social and activist actions outside the art field.

In the art field itself, this movement includes not just artistic practices but all the other activities performed in this field: curating, museum management, criticism, art history, etc. Curatorial practices whose line of inquiry aligns with the perspective I outlined above share a common thread: a will to promote the aforementioned disruption of the dominant cultural paradigm. This will is realized whenever the pulse of embryonic worlds contained in certain artistic practices is activated. Curatorial proposals manage to activate this pulse through their choice of works, through the composition they establish between these works, and through the spaces conceived to bring this composition into existence. And when a curatorial proposal manages to activate this pulse, conditions are created for it to pollinate the public of an art exhibit, activating the pulse of embryonic worlds already present in the bodies of this public. This, in turn, makes other germinations possible, beyond the restricted space of the art world.

Curatorial proposals that focus on art from the past also carry this power of pollination. When embryonic worlds are encoded in the genetics of an artwork from the past, the possibility of activating the pulse of these worlds and of pollinating the environment outlives both the moment that the artwork was created and the movements that originated it. The forms present in past artworks belong to the past, but the drive behind the creation of these works can be reactivated at any moment. What always remains possible is restarting the germination of embryonic futures that remain buried, interrupted. Activating this process in the present generates other scenarios, different from those of the past.

But nothing ensures that the potency carried by past, buried seeds of embryonic futures, will be actualized. This is because, in the realm of micropolitical resistances, nothing can be foreseen, much less guaranteed. Regardless of the realm of human activity where insurrection in the micropolitical sphere takes place, the clash between various degrees of active and reactive forces (in the process of defining the forms of the present) will always exist.

The Belief in Paradise Is Rubbish

In this sense, we must let go of the belief in the delirium of a permanent and definitive control over the social wheelwork, a control that could presumably lead to a full realization of the human potential. This is a belief that derives from notions of "salvation," themselves derived from Western monotheist religions and their idea of "paradise." The only difference is that, in the belief outlined above, paradise can and must be found in this life, and not in the afterlife. It's an idea that results from a politics of anthropo-phallo-ego-logocentric subjectivation, reduced to the subject and guided by the colonial-capitalistic unconscious. There's a denial in it of the clash resulting from the complex, paradoxical relationship between the plane of forces and the plane of forms. Such denial interrupts the process of germination of embryonic futures nesting in the body, for, as we saw before, when we stay attuned to this clash, desire is called upon to act, in the sense of creating conditions for the germination of new forms of expression, in a never-ending process.

In the sphere of micropolitical struggle, the image of paradise is the image of a world where life finally finds its supposedly eternal peace – a delirium concocted by reactive forces. In the sphere of macro struggle, the image of paradise has two versions: the paradise of equality without conflicts proper to a socialist society or the paradise of "free" competition of the liberal market. Both images, conceived after the first industrial revolution, deny the micropolitical sphere. In the case of the image of paradise harbored by the left – especially the more traditional left and, even more so, the institutionalized left – this denial is partly responsible for its aforementioned impotence vis-à-vis the present impasses of the colonial-capitalistic regime and its perverse operations in the micropolitical sphere.

Abandoning the idea of paradise as well as the idea of the apocalypse (two sides of the same coin) is one of the challenges of the micropolitical struggle against the colonial-capitalist regime, the struggle for a life freed from its pimping. This protest of the unconscious is a fight that never achieves the supposed jouissance of a grand finale, an expectation proper to a subjectivity reduced to the subject, to its ignorance of body-knowing (the knowing proper to all living beings), and to its consequent deliriums. To rise to the challenge of vital demands leads to a different kind of jouissance, dislodged from the demands of the ego: a vital jouissance.

And now, dear reader, the time has come to ask ourselves one last question: Where is the meaning of – and the taste for– a life that perseveres, insistently? Where is that meaning, if not in assuming the challenge of vital demands?

Macro- and Micropolitical Insurgency
Links and Dissimilarities

The exhaustion of natural resources is probably less advanced than the exhaustion of subjective resources, of vital resources, that is afflicting our contemporaries. If so much satisfaction is derived from surveying the devastation of the environment it's largely because this veils the shocking destruction of interiorities. Every oil spill, every sterile plain, every species extinction is an image of our souls in shreds, a reflection of our absence from the world, of our personal inability to inhabit it.

Comité Invisible[25]

It is the relationship between subjectivity and its exteriority – be it social, animal, vegetable or Cosmic – that is compromised in this way, in a sort of general movement of implosion and regressive infantilization. Otherness [l'altérité] tends to lose all its asperity.

Félix Guattari[26]

Our planet (and us with it) finds itself under the impact of voraciously destructive forces. Everywhere, there's a sense of general malaise; the sensations that launch us into that state are numerous. There is also, everywhere, a sense of perplexity; it emerges when we come face to face with the rise to power of the capitalist regime in its new fold (its financialized and neoliberal fold), which takes its colonial project to its logical conclusion, to its globalitarian realization. Aside from the perplexity we face when we confront this phenomenon, we are also overtaken by a sense of fright in the presence of another, simultaneous phenomenon: the rise of conservative forces, which contributes to the increased toxicity of the planetary atmosphere. These forces have taken root with such violence and such a level of barbarism that we cannot help but remember both the 1930s, the years before World War II, and also the decades after the war, when dictatorial regimes emerged in South America, in the Soviet Union, and elsewhere (the same regimes that dissolved over the course of the 1980s).[27] It is as if these forces never actually disappeared, as if they only made a strategic retreat, waiting for the right conditions for their triumphant return, reappearing in a loop that never seems to come to an end.

Neoliberalism and (Neo)conservatism

At first, the simultaneous appearance of these two phenomena (the rise of the capitalist regime in its new fold, the upsurge of conservative forces) seems paradoxical: they are radically distinct symptoms of the same reactive forces, as different as their respective historical groundings. The great degree of complexity, flexibility, and perverse sophistication characteristic of the neoliberal mode of existence (and of its strategies of power) is light years ahead of the small-minded archaism and the rigidness of the brute forces of neoconservatism. The "neo" in "neoconservatism" makes sense only as a function of the sociopolitical-economic conditions that it is geared for, conditions that differ from those that came along with older forms of the same conservatism.

Once the initial shock subsides, it becomes evident that financialized capitalism demands brute subjectivities in power, willing and able to do the dirty work needed for the enthronement of a neoliberal state. This dirty work has three objectives: to destroy every democratic and republican achievement; to dissolve the imaginary of these achievements; and to eradicate the protagonists of these achievements from the scene. Among these protagonists, those situated on the left, in its different gradations, are singled out for removal with notable eagerness.

We must note, however, that this removal includes anyone who stands in the way of the establishment of the neoliberal state. And if a new breed of old conservatives agrees to this task, it is because the interests of both neoliberals and neoconservatives converge on the three objectives outlined above, which must be fulfilled if the neoliberal state is to be established. This is what allows for a temporary alliance between neoliberalism and (neo)conservatism.

The brutish subjectivity of neoconservatives is intrinsically classist and racist, and this leads them to play their role without the slightest ethical consideration and with dizzying swiftness. Before we know it, before we even notice the piercing wound of one of its stabs, another stab is already on its way, usually by way of a Congress that votes on this new attack overnight, under the cloak of darkness. Fulfilling these duties brings neoconservatives perverse narcissistic pleasure, unscrupulous to the point of obscenity. Once this dirty work is pleasurably completed, the ground is prepared to expand as much as possible the free flow of transnational capital, the same kind of transnational capital now installed in Brazil.

Malaise Beyond the Tolerable: Trauma

The general air of malaise hardly stops here. Along with perplexity and fright comes a profound frustration with the current, cascading dissolution of several left-leaning governments throughout the world, especially in Latin America[28] – the result of the rise of reactive conservative and neoliberal forces, temporarily united. This frustration mobilizes a traumatic memory of deception linked to the grim destiny of twentieth-century revolutions, a deception aggravated when we confirm how impotent the left is in this new scenario.

Compounded, all these sensations – perplexity, fright, frustration, and deception – take malaise beyond the limit of tolerability. A state of alertness takes hold of subjectivity, the way it does whenever the lack of essential, vital resources reaches a point where life itself is at risk. When that happens, we are engulfed by an urgency that calls desire into action. The responses given by desire to those traumatic situations oscillate between two extreme poles: a reactive and pathological pole

62   Macro- and Micropolitical Insurgency

(where we lose potency) and an active pole (where our vital potency is not only preserved but tends to be intensified).

In the active response to trauma, the scope of our gaze expands in a way that allows us to be more capable of accessing the effects of violence on our bodies. This response allows us to decipher and express these effects more precisely, which in turn makes us more skillful in the invention of ways to combat the effects of violence. Insurgencies in the social scene begin to form in that experience, rehearsing new strategies as a function of the singular problems that sparked such uprisings. This is the nature of the insurgencies that are irrupting everywhere, introducing strategies in places where the left–right binary no longer works as a sufficient operator in the delineation of the forces that are at work, in places where this binary can no longer define the target of combat. What emerges are movements of insubordination that have coalesced first and foremost among the younger generations (especially in the outskirts of large urban centers, particularly among blacks, women, and LGBTQI people), among indigenous peoples, and in *quilombola* communities.[29]

That said, isn't it possible that these new insurrectional movements seem surprising precisely because of a change in strategy? Isn't it precisely *that* which fascinates us, regardless of how difficult *that* is to decipher and name? And isn't the existence of those movements what has saved us from capitulating to the melancholic and fatalist paralysis caused by the somber landscape that surrounds us? The target of struggle grows more complex in the emergent and increasingly populated territories defined by these movements. It now includes a displacement of the dominant politics of subjectivation. The horizon touched by this new modality of struggle expands the reach of our vision, allowing us to picture the sphere of the micropolitical more neatly. But how is the violence of the colonial-capitalistic[30] regime operated in that sphere?

The Abuse of Life

What characterizes, micropolitically, the colonial-capitalistic regime is the pimping of life as force of creation, of transmutation, and of variation – the essence of life and the condition

Macro- and Micropolitical Insurgency

for its persistence, which is itself the embodiment of life's ultimate purpose, of its ethical destiny. This desecrating rape of life is the micropolitical marrow of the colonial-capitalistic regime, and that's why we can call this regime a pimp: a pimp-colonial-capitalistic regime. What gets pimped here, what gets expropriated and corrupted, is the vital force of all the elements that constitute the biosphere: plants, animals, humans, and so forth. The three planes that make up the planetary ecosystem, the planes on which life depends for its composition and maintenance (the Earth's crust; the atmosphere; the oceans, rivers, all the bodies of water), are also pimped by this regime.

The vital force of every living species has specific characteristics. Freud referred to this force as "the drive" in human beings, thus indicating that it is particular to our species, and thus distinguishing it from what he called "instinct." The concept is central to psychoanalytic theory. For Freud, what is proper to human beings is language and its capacity for creation. What's proper to humans, according to Freud, is both language and the creating capacity intrinsic to language, which expands, according to him, the power of variation of forms of life. A lasting, anthropocentric, and naturalizing bias in Freud's thought is revealed both in his use of the word "instinct" as the generic term for the vital force of animals and in his view of language (and of the potency of creation proper to language) as something restricted to humans.[31]

If we want to sharpen our understanding of the specificity of the vital force, we must first recognize that all life forms carry an expressive and creating capacity. Therefore, it is misleading to classify the vital force of nonhuman living beings under the generic concept of "instinct," which suggests these other species are inferior to humans. That said, what is distinctive about the vital force in the human species is that the language that this species uses is more elaborate and more complex, which amplifies its power of variation but which can also, on the other hand, restrict this variation.

Relatedly, Freud notes in his writings on the drive that the expansion of the capacity for variation (in the concretization of this drive) can also lead to what he calls the "death drive."[32] This is not the place to ponder the nuances and complexities of that concept and the innumerable ways in which it has been interpreted. Besides, a vast bibliography on the subject already exists.

64 Macro- and Micropolitical Insurgency

What matters here is problematizing the use of the term "death" to qualify the destiny of the drive.

If, unlike Freud, we begin from the idea that the drive is always a life drive (or a "will to power," as Nietzsche's translators call it),[33] we are compelled to say that the destiny of the drive varies from the more active to the more reactive (or from the more noble to the more slavish, in keeping with terms proposed by Nietzsche). Thus seen, what Freud called the "death drive" would correspond to the maximum degree of reactivity of the life drive, its lowest degree of potency. We must highlight, however, that this destiny, too, is life: it is a will to potency. If this distinction makes any difference whatsoever, it is because forms in society result from the clash between variously active and variously reactive life forces. The dominant politics of subjectivation in any given historical moment depends on this clash, and this clash, in turn, always leaves open the possibility that the reactive destiny of the drive prevails, with grave consequences for the perseverance of life itself.[34]

In the colonial-capitalistic regime whose politics of subjectivation we want to decipher here, this is precisely the dominant tendency, which leads to an interruption of the processes of creation of new forms of life. This makes our species perhaps the only one that dares to intervene in these processes to the point of interrupting them, derailing the drive from its ethical destiny as it concerns human life. The effect of this derailment is the depotentializing of life, which nowadays amounts to the destruction of the very sources of vital energy of the biosphere – sources that, in humans, include the subjective resources of its preservation. If the tradition of Marxism, originated in industrial capitalism, brought us awareness of the fact that the expropriation of the vital force in humans (in its manifestation as labor force) is the source that feeds the accumulation of capital, the new version of capitalism leads us to recognize that this expropriation is not limited to that domain. This is because, in its newest fold, expropriation refines itself, which makes it more evident that the colonial-capitalistic regime feeds from the very provenance of the movement of the drive. Put another way, it feeds from the impetus to create forms of existence and cooperation where the demands of life become concrete, transfiguring the scenarios of the present and transvaluating its values.

Macro- and Micropolitical Insurgency

The drive is diverted by the colonial-capitalistic regime from this ethical destiny and channeled towards the construction of worlds made according to the regime's objectives, which center on capital accumulation: economic, political, cultural, and narcissistic capital accumulation. The assault on the vital force produces a trauma that numbs subjectivity vis-à-vis the demands of the drive. This leaves desire vulnerable to corruption: it stops being guided, in its actions, by the impetus to preserve life, and it even tends to act against life. Scenarios arise from that politics wherein life finds itself more and more deteriorated. That is what increases the current destruction of the planet to levels that threaten the very continuity of life on Earth. And this is precisely what the violence of the colonial-capitalist regime consists in at the level of the micropolitical: a cruelty on a par with its perverse politics of desire, subtle and refined, invisible in the eyes of our consciousness. It is a violence similar to the violence of the pimp who uses seduction to instrumentalize the labor force of his prey, in this case, the erotic force of his prey's sexuality. Under the spell of the pimp, the sex worker tends to ignore his cruelty. Instead, she tends to idealize him, which leads her willingly to give herself up to the abuse by virtue of her own desire. She can manage to free herself from that sad submission only when she breaks the spell caused by the idealization of her oppressor.

Breaking this perverse spell depends on her discovering that what lies behind the omnipotent appearance of power constructed by the pimp (power over himself and the world, which the sex worker interprets as a guarantee of her protection and safety) is, in fact, one of the most sordid forms of human misery. For the pimp, the other is a mere object for the narcissistic jouissance of accumulating power, prestige, and capital. This jouissance comes from the power to dominate the other and to instrumentalize her according to his wishes. The spell is broken when the sex worker realizes that the other – including and specially herself – is not perceived as an existence of its own in the eyes of the pimp, not even in the most minimal sense. When this fact is revealed, the sex worker begins to free herself from the dynamic of the unconscious that keeps her both a prisoner of her self-assigned role and an accomplice to the pimp. A process of transfiguration is thus unleashed. It brings down the whole scene.

66 Macro- and Micropolitical Insurgency

The perverse dynamic that guides the regime of the unconscious corresponding to the characters that compose the capitalist scene is similar to the one that holds between sex worker and pimp. To single out the specificity of this regime, I propose we refer to it as a "colonial-capitalistic unconscious."[35] If we want to be more precise, we can also refer to it as "pimp-colonial-capitalistic unconscious."

The Uncanny, or the Strange-Familiar: The Ineluctable Paradox of Subjective Experience

The main feature of this regime of the unconscious is the reduction of subjectivity to its experience as subject. But what does this experience entail? The function of the subject is intrinsic to the cultural condition corresponding to the human – it is shaped by its imaginary. It provides us with the ability to decipher the present-day forms of the society we belong to, its places and functions, the distribution of these places and functions and their relational dynamics, its codes, and its representations. This deciphering takes place in the practice of cognition made possible by intelligence and reason, based on what our capacities for perception (sensorial emotion) and feeling (psychological emotion) signal for us. These latter capacities are marked by the repertories of sociocultural representations that structure the subject and its language. We associate what we perceive and feel to certain representations, and we project these representations onto what we perceive, which allows us to classify and recognize what we perceive, defining it and producing meaning based on it.

In this sphere of subjective experience – sensorial, sentimental, and rational – the other is lived as an external body, as something separate from the subject. The relationship to the other is here given by means of communication, based on a shared language, which allows for reciprocal recognition. Habits are here constituted in the experience of the subject: they imprint on everyday life a spatial (concrete space) and temporal (chronological time) organization, which creates a feeling of familiarity. This is the sphere of the macropolitics of human life. The ability to access this sphere is essential to coexistence in society.

The problem of the regime of the colonial-capitalistic unconsciousness is the reduction of subjectivity to its experience as subject, which leaves out an experience immanent to our being alive: the experience outside-the-subject. For life, the consequences of this reduction are nefarious. But what exactly is that other sphere of subjective experience? As living beings, we are constituted by the effects of the forces of the vital flux and its diverse and mutating relationships, which agitate the forms of a world. The forces that give rise to these effects act singularly on every body that forms part of a world, human and nonhuman. These effects turn these bodies into one and the same body, in continuous variation, regardless of whether we are conscious of this or not. We can refer to these effects as "affects." What we're dealing with is an extrapersonal, extrasensorial, and extrasentimental experience. It is an extrapersonal experience because there is no personal boundary here, because here we are the changing effects of the forces of both the biosphere and of the other planes that make up the planet's ecosystem, forces that compose and recompose our bodies. It is an extrasensorial experience because it is given by means of affect, which is different from perception, itself corresponding to the plane of the sensorial. And it is an extrasentimental experience because it takes place by means of "vital emotion," which is different from the psychological emotion that we refer to as "sentiments" or "feelings."

The mode of deciphering that corresponds to the power of evaluation proper to affects is extracognitive – what we usually refer to as "intuition." The use of this word, however, often leads to misunderstandings in modern Western culture, which, in reducing subjectivity to the subject, spurns all modes of knowledge different from cognition, given that it operates under the rule of reason (the mode proper to the subject). Such disdain stems from and feeds into logocentrism, which is hegemonic in this cultural context. For this reason, I suggest replacing the term "intuition" by the term "body-knowledge," or knowledge proper to all living beings: an "eco-ethological" knowledge.

The medium of relation with the other in the subjective experience of the outside-the-subject is not communication (as is the case in the experience of the subject) but, rather, resonance (in the field of intensities). In this sphere of relation with the other, there is no distinction between cognizant subject and exterior object (the kind of distinction that holds in the experience of the subject). Here, the other effectively lives in our bodies, and it does so by means of affects: by means of the effects of its presence in us. These effects take place within the purview of a condition shared by humans with their others: being alive. This shared condition, in turn, renders humans and their others into one and the same body. When others are introduced into our body by the effects they have on it, the forces of the world enter into composition with the forces that already animate our body, fertilizing it.

This is how embryos of virtual worlds are generated, embryos that produce in us a sensation of estrangement. And this is the sphere of the micropolitics of human existence. Accessing this sphere is essential as we situate ourselves in relation to life and as we make choices that protect life and potentialize it. Meeting the demands of life depends on a process of creation that has its own temporality, different from the chronological time of the macropolitical sphere, whose rhythm is predetermined. Becomings of the self and of the world emerge from this process. It differs from the dynamic of the macropolitical sphere, where standing forms are repeated as a matter of principle.

The Malaise of Paradox Calls Forth the Action of Desire

The familiar and the strange, two totally different sensations that come to us from the experiences of the subject (the personal), on the one hand, and the experiences of the outside the subject (the extrapersonal), on the other hand, work simultaneously and indissociably. But they work according to disparate temporalities, disparate logics, and disparate dynamics. There is absolutely no possibility of a conciliatory synthesis between them, nor is it possible for one to be translated into the other. On the contrary, the relationship between them is characterized by a paradox that is ineluctable as a matter of principle. What we are dealing with here are embryonic futures setting off the drive-movement of their germination, which leads life to take shape in other forms of the world. These forms are designed not in opposition to the present forms but in affirmation of becomings, the effects of which constitute a threat to the continuity of present forms.

Destabilized by the paradoxical experience of the uncanny, of the strange-familiar, subjectivity finds itself tensed between two movements. On the one hand, the movement described

Macro- and Micropolitical Insurgency

above pressures it in the direction of the conservation of life in its potency of germination, so that it embodies new modes of existence. On the other hand, there is a movement that pressures it in the direction of the conservation of the present modes, where life finds itself temporarily materialized and where subjectivity finds a sense of familiarity, where it is used to recognizing its experience as subject. The malaise caused by the tension between both the strange and the familiar and also between the two movements unleashed by that paradoxical experience is what puts subjectivity in a state of alert, in much the same way as it happens today. This is because this malaise triggers an alarm that calls desire into action, so that vital, emotional, and existential equilibrium is once again reached – an equilibrium unsettled by the signals of a nascent world, which are simultaneous to and inseparable from the signals sent by present worlds in the process of dissolving. A constant negotiation between these two movements is imposed upon desire.

It is precisely at this point that different politics of desire are defined, from the most active to the most reactive. What distinguishes these micropolitics is the type of negotiation (between the aforementioned movements) that desire will privilege in its actions. The choice is not a neutral one, because hinging on that choice are different destinies for the drive. They entail different formations of the unconscious in the social field, which carry more or less vigor in their affirmation of life. This is the micropolitical ground upon which every socio-political-economic regime acquires its existential consistency. The battlefield proper to the micropolitical sphere takes shape as a function of the clash between different politics of desire.

The Colonial-Capitalistic Unconscious

A reactive micropolitics prevails over subjectivities governed by the colonial-capitalistic unconsciousness, reduced as they are to their experience as subject. In them, the movement for the conservation of the present forms of existence tends to be dominant. Subjectivity in this case lives the pressure of embryonic worlds as a threat of disaggregation, of itself and of its relational field, dissociated as it is from the condition proper to all living beings, and neglecting as it does the continuous process of mutation

70   Macro- and Micropolitical Insurgency

corresponding to the vital dynamic (a drive dynamic or dynamic of the drive, in human beings). This is because "this world," the world where the subject lives and where its current self-image is based, is lived by it as if it was "*the* world," the one and only world.

Under these conditions, and in hopes of regaining its equilibrium, desire clutches onto pre-established forms and seeks to preserve them at all costs. The more the subject is unsettled, the more vehemently it shelters itself inside what is already instituted, defending it fiercely, tooth and nail, to guarantee its permanence. This defense can be violent to the point of killing anyone – any other – who does not mirror the subject and whose existence shakes its confidence in the absolute universality of its own world.

The separation of subjectivity from its condition as living being prepares the ground for desire to surrender itself gleefully to the pimping of the drive, whose movements desire executes. This surrender is evinced in the reduction of the drive's potency to "create" new modes of existence (in response to the demands of life) to mere "creativity," which is placed in the service of the composition of new scenarios for the accumulation of capital. Instead of the creation of the new, "novelties" are produced "creatively" and compulsively, which multiplies the opportunities for capitalist investments and stimulates the itch for consumption. In other words, the vital potency is redirected and used for the reproduction of the instituted. The different pieces of what's already instituted are shuffled around or slightly altered in a more or less creative way. Under crisis, the redirection of the drive and the surrender of desire to its own abuse are intensified. This is evident in mass movements that call for maintaining the status quo, as is the case in the blistering rise of conservatism we have recently witnessed. The subject's joy derives from the same illusion under both types of reactive, desiring action – creation reduced to creativity; conservative movements – that emerge in response to the experience of the strange-familiar. It is an illusion rooted in a false sense of its stability and belonging, a kind of placebo against the fear of stigmatization and social shame that the destabilization of its world causes in the subject when it interprets this destabilization as impending collapse.

The result of these types of actions by desire is a baleful destiny for the drive: the interruption of the process of germination of

Macro- and Micropolitical Insurgency

collective life. The reason why this process is interrupted at the level of collective existence is simple. Even when germination stalls only at the level of the existence of an individual or a group, it necessarily generates a point of putrefaction in the life of the social body, as well as in the life of the environment. This is one example of the dominant politics of subjectivation where the referred tendency to act against life is evident.

It is difficult to grasp the desecrating abuse of the drive. This is because it takes place in a sphere beyond consciousness, and because the experience of this abuse is numbed in the hegemonic mode of subjectivation, under the spell of a perverse seduction that captivates the subject. Nonetheless, the innumerable manifestations of this abuse in the social field are plainly accessible to those who manage to stay attentive to the processes that degrade life, evident as they are in every symptom of the violation of life. To cite but some of the most obvious symptoms of the desecrating abuse of the drive, we can highlight the relationships with the environment that result in disaster. We can also point to power relations contingent upon classism, sexism, homophobia, transphobia, racism, xenophobia, chauvinism, nationalism, colonialism, and so forth. In all these manifestations of the abuse of the drive, the subject casts the other in an imaginary role: as an object in the service of the subject. These are power relations defined by pimping.

There is a second class of symptoms characterized by an additional aspect, symptoms where the abuse is supported by an imaginary that projects onto that other – the other reduced to being an object – a supposedly inferior, even subhuman nature. This projection can result in an utter and complete erasure of the other, producing its inexistence to a degree that, as mentioned above, is equal to their extermination, and that in extreme cases can also culminate in the disappearance of the other's very body. This is what Nazis referred to as "The Final Solution," thus signaling the moment when its politics of relating to the other reached its most extreme and radical explicitness, with the use of gas chambers and cremation ovens. With variations in procedures, this "solution" was later adopted by, among other regimes, the dictatorial governments that emerged in Latin America in the 1960s, 1970s, and 1980s. One such variation in procedure consisted in tying up people or drugging them unconscious, placing them on airplanes or helicopters,

72 Macro- and Micropolitical Insurgency

and then dropping them over oceans, rivers, and mountains (this procedure generated the category of *desaparecidos*, which applies to those whose bodies have never been found).

These examples of the desecrating abuse of life cannot be considered epiphenomenal relative to a regime. They are symptoms of the regime, symptoms of its constitutive and guiding principle, of its dominant politics of desire and subjectivation. Because of this, it is evidently not enough to subvert the roles of the characters at play in the scene of power relations that makes the desecrating abuse of life possible, the way this scene is subverted in macropolitical insurrection. It is also necessary to simultaneously insurrect in the micropolitical sphere. In other words, it is necessary to abandon these roles and their politics of desire. This derails the continuity of the scene itself, in the same way that it is derailed when the spell of power cast by the pimp on the subjectivity of his prey is broken.

Though they function under different logics and different temporalities, uneven and paradoxical, insurgency against violence in both the macro- and micropolitical spheres depends, invariably, on the dissolution of the regime everywhere and in every human activity. This is the sine qua non for an effective transmutation of the present, because, in its most recent version, the regime managed to colonize the planet as a whole, affecting all its entrails, macro- and micropolitically, to the point that no human activity is beyond its purview. That's why Guattari began referring to this regime at the beginning of the 1980s as "Integrated World Capitalism,"[36] when the regime was just starting to show its symptoms. The Brazilian geographer Milton Santos,[37] for his part, referred to it as "globalitarian capitalism." This new scene allows us to see the reason behind the impotence of the left (especially of the more traditional left and, even more pointedly, of the institutionalized left) – vis-à-vis the challenges of the present. What used to be called "resistance" in this tradition has been reduced to the macropolitical sphere, which limits both the scope of its vision and the success of its strategies.

Why Does the Left Seem So Lost Today?

First and foremost, we must recognize that, even if the swing to right-wing politics at the level of state power contributes to the impotence of the left, this impotence cannot be explained as the mere result of external, adverse forces. Its cause is also internal. Herein lies what is perhaps its greatest challenge, which threatens its ability to fight against external forces. What I'm suggesting is that, because the traditional left acts exclusively in the field of the forms of reality and its organization, their politics of subjectivation are in no way different than the politics of the other subjects in the colonial-capitalistic regime, given that it is in that regime that the left originated and where it has unfolded over the course of the years. What follows from the reduction of these actions of the left to the macropolitical sphere is that these actions remain confined to the very form of the world that its (that our) struggle takes as its principal target. The perspective that guides the various kinds of leftist struggle tend, therefore, to perpetuate the logic of the same regime that they (that we) want to overcome. It is, then, hardly unexpected that the actions of these leftist struggles tend to result in the sad and frustrating reproduction of the regime that they are supposed to overturn.

Without a doubt, the position taken by the left in the macropolitical sphere of this regime is the fairest one. This is because, through different procedures, the actions of the left seek a more equitable distribution in the social, economic, and political domains, which involves fighting for a state that sustains this expansion of equality. And it is a fact that, in different magnitudes and for different stretches of time, this objective has been reached on several occasions. The struggle that culminates in these conquests is undoubtedly indispensable, and it has undeniable value. The problem, however, is that, when it remains exclusively focused on these conquests, the left stays out of the struggle in the micropolitical sphere, where the formations of the unconscious are produced. This, in turn, produces a prevalence of a certain politics of subjectivation and of its respective politics of desire (it's worth remembering that these micropolitics constitute the existential base of every sociopolitical-economic-cultural regime).

Even when the left, especially the traditional left, does manage to grapple with modes of existence, it tends to do so from an exclusively macropolitical perspective. These modes of existence are then classified as identities, which completely confine the subjectivities that practice such modes of existence. Subjectivities then tend to confuse themselves with identitarian entities, which

74   Macro- and Micropolitical Insurgency

leads them to waste the micropolitical potency of their mode of existence, limiting their resistance to the macropolitical sphere. This is particularly worrisome when it happens among vulnerable social segments, where the struggles of the left have historically taken place. In the industrial fold of capitalism, these segments, in all their diversity, were usually homogenized by the left under the category of "workers."

"Worker" became a fetishized identitarian category, intended for the oppressed in the imaginary of the left because this imaginary was (and continues to be) limited both to class relations and to the visions of the world that originated in this fold of the regime. It is also limited to the vision of insurrection that originated in that same fold of the regime. When it comes to segments of society that cannot be forced into this category (indigenous people, for instance, as well as *quilombolas*, gig economy workers, subcontracted workers, migrants, undocumented people, and refugees), what the traditional left does is to promote "inclusion" in the official map of democracy in such way that these sectors can access the rights of workers.[38] Accessing civil rights is, of course, essential, but reducing the struggle to that goal leads the left to a denial of the singularity of these segments of society, converting this singularity into a kind of identitarian cartoon. And when these identitarian cartoons are embraced by these very segments of society, they tend to lead to a submissive adoption of the hegemonic mode of subjectivation. This is the phenomenon that the left refers to as "inclusion."

The call for "inclusion" as the main (and sometimes only) goal reveals not only that the traditional left does, in fact, tend to embrace the dominant cartography as its point of reference. It also indicates that this left considers the dominant cartography as *the* point of reference, absolute and universal, the standard against which all modes of existence should be measured and with which they should identify if they are to prosper. This is because, from the perspective of the dominant cartography – shared, in this sense, by the left itself – differences in every mode of existence in relation to its own mode of existence are seen as indicators of backwardness in the so-called civilizing process, the presumed destiny of the whole of humanity. The singular experience of subjectivities is thus neutralized, and any alterity is also denied.

Even worse, this also brings about the loss of an indispensable experience: inhabiting the relational plot of the different modes of existence and also, most importantly, experiencing the transforming effects that can emerge from this (an experience which renders the dominant cartography obsolete). What gets quashed when this view is limited to the macropolitical sphere is a chance for the vital force to fulfill its ethical destiny, a chance for it to invent responses that meet the need for change that arises precisely from the effects that human and nonhuman alterity has on the bodies that make up the fabric of society. In sum, what gets quashed is an emergence of becomings: the becomings of collective life, proper to micropolitical insubordination, which can emerge from these effects.

Faced with an exclusively macropolitical gaze that reduces everything to class relations, when these becomings take place and new modes of existence emerge from collective life, they are seen by the left through the same lens it uses to see the components of society that don't fit its categories. The left tends to confine these becomings to new identitarian entities, which then multiply, endlessly, reproducing the same logics. This is how the left reacts to the movements that are now expanding the sphere of sexual experimentation and disturbing notions such as gender and heteronormativity – notions that, under patriarchy, guide the hegemonic practices in that sphere. These notions confine and homogenize erotic force, with no regard for the possibility of variation and transfiguration in this force, which is indispensable for social and individual health (and which is also indispensable for the vital force in all its manifestations in human existence, and not just in its manifestation in sexuality).

When the left ignores the processes of singularization taking place in the insurgencies that agitate this domain, it neutralizes the transmutating effects such insurgencies have on the hegemonic politics of subjectivation. It also neutralizes the changes to the forms of individual and collective existence that result from these transmutations. In sum, what gets ignored and neutralized is the potency of micropolitical combat that these movements carry with them. Even though some currents within the left do recognize and value the existence of these movements, they tend to reduce them to questions about equal rights, remitting the focus of their insurrection to the struggles between oppressor and oppressed, following the model of class struggle. This can be seen in the academic world, where a segment of intellectuals scattered across the leftist spectrum insist on analyzing the changes operated by these new kinds of insurgencies, but confining their thought to a strictly macropolitical perspective. What comes out of this is nothing more than sterile rumination. We see this in the tendency of certain scholarly analyses of the current situation, which obsessively return to the question of the crisis of democracy, with the state as the central focus and the question of how to reform the state (so as to better represent the people) as the main concern.

The fact that the left limits its horizon to the sphere of macropolitics can be explained as follows. Because it remains under the rule of hegemonic modes of existence, its subjectivity tends to be reduced to its experience as subject. What is more, the left also tends to reduce the subjectivity of others to their experience as subjects. Therein lies the origin of the left's inability to access the sphere of micropolitics. In the end, the reason behind the impotence of the left vis-à-vis emerging challenges is the politics of desire that tends to prevail in its own subjectivity: a micropolitics guided by the colonial-capitalistic unconsciousness.

Recognizing this fact is already a huge step forward. It keeps those of us who stand with the left from remaining paralyzed, lamenting melancholically either the impotence of the left when faced with the new fold of capitalism or our frustrations with governments formed under this fold, in the past or in the present. This recognition, however, is not enough: we must take a step forward. We must explore pragmatically and theoretically the sphere of micropolitics, because, without the reappropriation of life, there is no chance for an effective transformation of the situation we find ourselves in, and there is also no chance for a transvaluation of its values. Equally urgent is the task of exploring the differences between, on the one hand, the drive-protest of the unconsciousnesses[39] that seeks to free life from its expropriation (micropolitical insurrection) and, on the other hand, the pragmatic protest of consciousnesses that seeks to expand the equality promoted through rights (macropolitical insurrection). Moreover, we must explore pragmatically and theoretically the inextricable link between these two insurrections in a way that allows us to adjust the focus of our strategies in both spheres. What follows are some notes in that direction.

What's the Difference between Macro- and Micropolitical Insurrection?

Let's summarize the principal aspects of an insurrection in order to examine their specificity in both macropolitical and micropolitical resistance. Greater attention will be placed on the specifically micropolitical aspects of resistance, because we have less accumulated experience on this front and because, moreover, it is in this sphere that we face our greatest challenge today: creating tools appropriate for the task of decolonizing the unconscious (the matrix of micropolitical resistance).

1) Focus

Macropolitics (a visible and audible focus, accessible on the subject side of subjective experience)
As outlined above, the focus of macropolitical insurrection is inequity in the distribution of rights corresponding to the cartography of social forms established by the colonial-capitalistic regime. In other words, its sharpest targets are the asymmetries in the power relations that are manifested not just between social classes but also between races, genders, sexualities, religions, ethnicities, and colonialities. Identifying these relations as the points of struggle involves the state as well as the laws that maintain these asymmetries.

Micropolitics (an invisible and inaudible focus, accessible in the experience of the tension between the subject and the outside-the-subject)
As it is also outlined above, the focus of micropolitical insurrection is the perverse abuse of the vital force of all the elements of the biosphere: the whole set of living beings that live on the planet, including humans. The abuse extends to the three spheres (hydrosphere, atmosphere, lithosphere) of the Earth's ecosystem that are indispensable for life and its preservation. This abuse is the micropolitical marrow of the regime of the colonial-capitalistic unconscious. The hegemony of its micropolitical dynamic constitutes a highly aggressive pathology with grave consequences not just for the destiny of humanity but for the entire planet, because it affects the four spheres of its ecosystem.

78 Macro- and Micropolitical Insurgency

2) Potential agents

Macropolitics (human agents only)
The only potential agents of macropolitical insurrection are human beings (as this sphere of uprising involves the state), especially those who occupy subaltern positions in the fabric of society. Nonetheless, consciousness of the inequity in the distribution of rights, as well as the will to fight this inequity, can also emerge from those who occupy sovereign positions in the web of power relations.

Micropolitics (humans and nonhuman agents)
Potential agents of micropolitical insurgency include all the elements of the biosphere that break out in revolt when they resist violence against life. There are, of course, different dynamics corresponding to the human and nonhuman elements of this insurrection and their respective response to that violence. Nonhuman elements are sensitive to the vital anemia caused by the abuse imposed upon them, and they tend to come up with transfigurations that allow life to regain its pulse. One example of this is a river that dries up when too much colonial-capitalistic waste is dumped on it. The river can be said to insurrect when it responds to this situation by taking shelter underground,[40] where it once again finds conditions to flow, free from the poisonous effects of this waste. Another example is trees that bloom out of season, rebelling against the risk of sterility that comes with the buildup of pollution.

Human elements of the biosphere, on the other hand, respond to the abuse of life as a function of desire, the dominant politics of which vary according to each culture, in its different moments and contexts. In the culture proper to the colonial-capitalistic regime (whose logic remains the same over time, with adjustments in its different folds), the reduction of subjectivity to the subject (which is inseparable from the abuse of the drive) generates a trauma. In the wake of this trauma there tends to prevail a reactive response – the grounds for the politics of subjectivation hegemonic under that regime.

As mentioned above, the state of fragility brought about by the abuse of life tends to be interpreted as a signal of our own flaws: egotistic, existential, and/or social flaws. This frightens us and, in the presence of this imaginary threat, reactive responses

Macro- and Micropolitical Insurgency

tend to prevail. Desire then latches onto the status quo, acting to conserve it and thereby acting against the perseverance of life, instead of operating in its favor. The formations of the unconscious in the social field that follow from this are responsible for the hordes of zombies that walk the Earth in increasingly terrifying ways.

But when, in this context of adversity, desire manages to respond actively to the trauma of abuse, desire potentializes, and it seeks to act towards decolonizing the unconscious, looking for ways to direct the vital drive away from the fate that capitalist pimping imposes on it. Subjectivity then gains a chance to live out the experience of the subject and the outside-the-subject simultaneously, in a quest to take back into its own hands the power to decide the destiny of the drive, assuming its ethical responsibility vis-à-vis life. It is through that very process that we turn into agents of micropolitical insurrection. Given the fact that decolonizing the unconscious necessarily entails the realm of our relations – from the most intimate to the more distant ones – the effects of any gesture in the direction of micropolitical insurrection are collective in nature.

Because we are all under the rule of the regime of the colonial-capitalistic unconscious, regardless of our place in the social, economic and cultural cartography, to be an agent of micropolitical insurgency does not depend on the position (more or less sovereign, more or less subaltern) we occupy in the web of power relations that constitutes that cartography. This may seem strange from a macropolitical point of view, and it may seem even more strange when our horizon is reduced to that sphere.

On the other hand, it is clear that, because everything that is lived at the level of forms and their codes is also and inextricably lived at the level of the forces that animate these forms and codes (and that also disorganize them, leading to their transfiguration), different subject positions in the relations of power in the macropolitical sphere (positions defined by class, race, ethnic, gender relations, and so forth) correspond to distinct experiences in the micropolitical sphere. It is important to note that there is no symmetry or parallel between potential agents of insurrection in either one of those spheres.

If, in the macropolitical sphere, these agents are distributed on a cartography organized in binary pairs (with the subaltern pole being the agent of insurrection par excellence), the logic

80 Macro- and Micropolitical Insurgency

of the distribution of these agents in the micropolitical diagram of forces is different, and it can emerge from any place in the fabric of society, because all of us are under the domain of the pimp-colonial-capitalistic unconscious. Faced with this fact, it is worth asking whether the effects that the abuse of the drive has on subalternized subjects are different than the effects it has on subjectivities that occupy the place of the sovereign. If this is the case, what is the nature of this difference?

When it comes to subalterns, both oppression and exploitation, as well as exclusion (which take place in the sphere of the macropolitical), produce, in the subjects who suffer from them, an experience of their existence as something worthless. This, in turn, generates an intolerable feeling of humiliation, which has, for the subject, a traumatic effect in the sphere of the micropolitical: it has the tendency to bruise even further a vital drive already weakened by the fear of a collapse of the self (a fear caused by the abuse). Class traumas, racial traumas, and ethnic traumas are among the most difficult traumas to overcome. They are constantly reaffirmed, from the beginning of an individual's life (which includes its family and community life) up to the very end. Moreover, these traumas date back to a time before birth, because they are inherited from one's ancestors and inscribed into one's DNA. They include far-removed experiences of colonization and slavery, the forced exile entailed by these experiences, the extermination of those who could not or did not adapt to forms of extreme power, and the (voluntary or involuntary) death of those who could not tolerate the inextricable, anemic state that these experiences cause in them (an anemic state so frequent among slaves brought to Brazil that the Angolan term used to describe this kind of death, "banzo," was adopted in Portuguese).[41]

The gravest thing is that these inherited traumas never stop being actualized. They're reproduced continuously, to this day. A double trauma – fear of collapse generated by the abuse of the vital drive; terror of humiliation generated by the disqualification that comes with the place society assigns to certain lives – threatens the integrity of life to such a degree that the responses produced by desire (regardless of whether they are most active or most reactive) tend to be intensified. The reactive response in subalternized subjects is a psychic defense strategy that further restricts their access to body-knowing in order to protect them from the toxic effects of trauma. This tends to prevent desire

Macro- and Micropolitical Insurgency

from acting in the direction of freeing itself from the colonization of the unconscious, which can, in turn, lead to an even greater submission both to the abuse of the drive and to oppression. The ranks of the underprivileged that fervently support political figures such as Jair Bolsonaro in Brazil,[42] or that make absurd demands for things such as the return of the military dictatorship, are very eloquent examples of this kind of reactivity.

The same threat to integrity can also, and on the contrary, generate an active response. It can move subalternized subjects to reconnect with body-knowing, as a matter of life or death. This, in turn, leads them to rip off the veil of phantasmatic narratives woven from their double trauma, narratives that mask the cause of their malaise and blur their vision of reality, leading them to the wrong actions. What moves them in this direction is the desire to take back the reins of the vital drive. When this takes place, these subjects tend to become stronger and more lucid, increasing their ability to resist (micropolitically) both abuse and humiliation and also (macropolitically) oppression, exploitation, and exclusion.

As far as the sovereign subject is concerned, the fear of collapse that comes from the abuse of the drive does not bring about a traumatic experience of humiliation linked to class and/or race. The alarm rings less stridently in the sovereign's subjectivity, and so the level of alertness triggered by the alarm – alertness in the face of a threat to life – is lower. But desire's response, in this case, oscillates equally across the range of micropolitics stretching between the two extreme poles (active and reactive) of possible destinies for the drive.

The reactive response originates from a decrease in desire's movement towards insurrection, which can lead to the triumph of a micropolitics that submits the vital drive to the whims of a subjectivity reduced to its gaze as subject. A response like this is reactive even if the gaze in question is (macro)politically correct. This reactive tendency is intensified by the material and narcissistic comfort that the sovereign position enjoys in the relations of power – the opposite of the place of discomfort that the subaltern is forced to occupy. All this leads sovereign subjectivity to hold on even tighter to established forms out of fear of losing its material privileges, which it tends to confuse with what it believes to be the vital privilege of its mode of existence. It is a mistake grounded on the imaginary of colonial-capitalistic

82   Macro- and Micropolitical Insurgency

societies, which elevates this mode of existence to the rank of the ideal that all of us should aspire to attain. In fact, this mode of existence corresponds to a sterile life, and it therefore does not constitute any kind of privilege. On the contrary, it is pathetically miserable. In this respect, the sovereign subject differs from the subaltern subject: in the sphere of the macropolitical, the subaltern has nothing to lose and everything to gain.

On the other hand, the very fact that the level of alertness is lower in the subjectivity of the sovereign subject can expand its psychic conditions so that it does not surrender to the trauma of the abuse, and so that desire gains enough momentum to confront this trauma micropolitically by means of an active response. When this takes place, desire connects with eco-ethological knowing. It is then guided by this knowing as it tries to free the drive from its pimping. In other words, privileged material conditions can, in this case, facilitate change instead of stalling it, and when this happens, desire acts towards creative practices. Until recently, these creative practices were often and primordially carried out in the field of art. But today these same practices are being carried out with more and more frequency as transfigurations of modes of existence. This includes the investment of desire in activist movements erupting in everyday life under oppression (in domains defined by gender, sexuality, race, ethnicity, etc.). It is worth noting, though, that, because of the reasons outlined above, when these kinds of transfigurations and movements take place in the marginalized parts of urban centers, they tend to be much fiercer, much more daring.

In the field of art, this is the context that gives rise to a renewed interest in the question of art and politics, which once again comes to the fore, though with renewed urgency and with a sense of radicality mobilized by the terrible situation of the planet. This time, however, the focus is less on works of art (and the challenge these works face in problematizing the art system from within, as was the case in the 1960s) and more on the following questions: How to resist the pimping of the potency of creation in art, which is to say, the pimping of its micropolitical potency? How can art strategies intervene beyond the sphere of institutionalized art, installing spaces that summon and support processes of experimentation and promote the proliferation of these processes as well as their respective becomings? Even more radically, how to contribute to the emancipation of the potency of creation from its confinement not only in the spaces intended for art but in the very category of "art"?

Of course, there's no generalizing when it comes to the realm of subjectivities. The figures outlined above, which embody active and reactive responses to abuse, overlap to different extents, thus composing different politics of desire that change over time. This is true for subjects in either a subaltern or a sovereign position. The dynamics of these figures in the micropolitical sphere are more complex and paradoxical than the positions each one occupies macropolitically in the social web. Nothing guarantees that all subalterns are, as a matter of principle, potential agents of micropolitical subordination, because their subjectivity may well be under the spell of the unconscious proper to the dominant regime, even when they fight this regime macropolitically. The reverse is also true: the sovereign subject can eventually turn into a micropolitically active agent if the spell of the values proper to the unconscious that rules the dynamics of that subject's class identification is broken in its subjectivity. This is true even when this subject doesn't go further than whatever is considered "politically correct" about its actions in the macropolitical field.

3) The Impulse That Moves These Agents

Macropolitics
What moves the agents of macropolitical insurrection is the will to "denounce," in words and actions, the injustices inherent to the distribution of rights in the present forms of the world. What these agents seek to achieve is to "raise awareness" in society by conveying information and formulating explanations in a way that mobilizes some of its sectors into action (especially the oppressed sectors by means of *identification* with other subalternized elements of society). In sum, what moves macropolitical agents is the will to *empower* both subalterns and macropolitical movements and their organizations, thereby intensifying and expanding their collective strength with the intent of establishing a more equitable distribution of rights.

Micropolitics
What moves the agents of micropolitical insurrection is the will to persevere that corresponds to life itself, a will that, in humans, is manifested as the impulse to *announce* worlds to come, in a

process of creation and experimentation that seeks to express these worlds. Embodied in words and actions that carry the pulse of these seeds of the future, this announcement tends to *mobilize other unconsciousnesses* by means of *resonances* with future embryos nesting in other bodies. New allies are thus added to the insubordination in the micropolitical sphere; these allies, for their part, are likely to throw themselves into other processes of experimentation. In those processes, other becomings of the world will be realized, different and unforeseeable from the perspective of those who mobilized them.

4) Intention

Macropolitics (empowering the subject)
The intention to insurrect macropolitically is the "empowering" of the subject, so that it frees itself from political oppression, from economic exploitation and social exclusion; so that it breaks its silence and undoes its invisibilization; so that it speaks up and so that others listen to it with the dignity it deserves; so that it occupies a duly recognized "place of existence." Because macropolitical insurrection seeks to promote a more equitable distribution of positions within the web of power relations, the intention behind the empowerment of the subject has as its ultimate objective the institution of a more democratic state.

Micropolitics (potentialization of life)
The intention of micropolitical insurrection is the "potentialization" of life: the reappropriation of the vital force in its creating potency. In humans, the reappropriation of the drive depends on the reappropriation of language (verbal, visual, gestural, existential, and other such expressions of language).

This, in turn, entails inhabiting the two dimensions of language: on the one hand, the form of expression of the subject and, on the other hand, the forces that compose the outside-the-subject, which bring movement to language and transform it. It entails, most of all, inhabiting the tension that results from the paradoxical relation between these two dimensions. The possibility of hurling oneself into a process of experimentation – a process fueled by this tension – depends on this. In this process, what guides desire is this tension: it guides it towards the expression (in words, images, gestures, modes of existence, modes of sexuality, etc.) of the embryonic worlds that disclose themselves to body-knowing.

Ultimately, there are two fundamental differences between the respective intentions of micropolitical and macropolitical struggles. First: expressing (in words and living actions) worlds that are emerging (which is proper to micropolitical insurrection) requires "implication" in that emergence, which is to say, it requires more than just an "explanation" that protects us and brings us imagined relief. This is a condition necessary for the drive-movement to complete its ethical destiny, producing an event. Second: *potentializing a life* is different from "empowering the subject," the latter being an intention corresponding to the macropolitical sphere of insurrection. Both intentions are important and complementary. The problem comes when the empowerment of the subject alone is pursued. In this case, the potentialization of life, which depends on desire's investment in the emergence of embryonic worlds, is disregarded. The result of this reduction is that we remain captive in the logic of the system we set out to combat.

Distinguishing between these intentions is especially necessary for bodies considered less valuable in the social imaginary – the poor body, the worker's body, the black body, the indigenous body, the female body, homosexual, transsexual, and transgender bodies, and so forth. When the insurgency of these bodies includes a desire for vital potency, over and above the empowerment of subjects, what is likely to happen is that the drive-movement finds its singular expression, and that it produces effective transmutations of individual and collective reality.

5) Criteria for Evaluating Situations

Macropolitics (moral criterion)
The criterion used in the sphere of micropolitics to evaluate situations is exclusively rational and guided by the moral judging characteristic of the subject. What guides choices and actions in the macropolitical sphere is a "moral compass." Its needle points to systems of values corresponding to current modes of existence: the modes with which each subjectivity identifies in its experience as subject, the ones it uses to situate itself within the social field.

Micropolitics (drive-criterion and its ethics)

The criterion used in the micropolitical sphere to evaluate situations is a "drive-criterion." What guides our choices and actions in the micropolitical sphere is an "ethical compass." Its needle points to what life imposes as a condition for its perseverance every time life begins to wane, suffocated by the present modes of existence and their values (which lose meaning when this happens). In sum, the micropolitical criterion for deciphering situations is guided by the power of evaluation corresponding to affects, which can be accessed in the experience outside-the-subject.

6) Modes of Operation

Macropolitics (by negation)

Insurrection in the macropolitical sphere operates by means of negation. It is combat *against* oppressors and against the laws that uphold their power in all its manifestations, in individual and collective life. This is the condition necessary to subvert the distribution of positions within relationships marked by oppression and exploitation. If the struggle here operates by way of opposition, this is because the interests of the two combating poles within the web of power relations are, in fact, opposite, which makes the dynamic of their struggle dialectical.

Micropolitical (by affirmation)

Insurrection in the macropolitical sphere operates by means of affirmation. It is a combat *for* life in its germinating essence. It consists in not giving in to the abuse of the drive, and it is contingent upon an extensive labor: working through the trauma of this abuse, the effects of which include the depotentializing of the vital drive, which prepares the ground for its pimping. The objective of this operating mode, corresponding to micropolitical struggle, is to neutralize – to the greatest extent possible, in each moment and everywhere they appear – the effects of the trauma of the abuse of the drive. Resisting this abuse is a necessary condition for disarticulating the power that the colonial-capitalistic unconscious has over our own subjectivities, a power that keeps us tangled up in the web of power relations, either in the position of the subaltern (even when we insurrect, macropolitically, against this position) or in the position of the sovereign

Macro- and Micropolitical Insurgency   87

(even when we proceed in a more or less macropolitically correct way).

Take, for example, women's struggles. Women's insurrection against inequalities in gender relations is indispensable and nondeferrable. That said, if women's insurrection is limited to the abandonment of their subaltern position in the sphere of macropolitics, there is nothing to guarantee that their subjectivity recovers its full existence, because that depends on reappropriating the drive, whose destiny has been sequestered by that same web of power relations. If women do not insurrect in the micropolitical sphere, they will likely remain dependent on a male gaze to feel themselves existing. In that way, women not only remain subject to the pitfalls of male domination and sexist abuse; they also continue to feed this domination with their own desire. In other words, if women's struggles do not incorporate the micropolitical sphere, these struggles tend to remain confined to a logic of opposition to men. Women's struggles then transform into a power dispute that takes the male character in the sexist scene as the only reference for their own identification. In this case, the hegemony of the male character is maintained, and so is the sexist scene that comes with it – precisely everything that women sought to fight in their macropolitical struggle.

The sexist scene, like any scene defined by power relations, is held up by two characters: the oppressor and the oppressed, both protagonists in the dynamic of this scene and both implied in it. To disarticulate this dynamic, the oppressed must leave behind the role assigned to it in this scripted abuse: either a victim of the oppressor or, in the best of cases, the opposite of the oppressor. The oppressed must then transfigure itself into other characters, or, better yet, it must leave the scene of abuse entirely. When this happens, the character of the oppressor, the scene partner of the oppressed, stays behind, talking to himself, and the show cannot go on. Isn't it exactly *this* insurrectional operation, in the sphere of micropolitics, what the social movements mentioned above have introduced? And isn't this particularly true in relation to the webs of power relations defined by race, sex, and gender?

But what happens with the character to which the oppressor finds itself confined when the character of the oppressed (the other lead character in this scene of power relations) is transfigured? Let's look further into the example of the sexist scene. Different men (who until then could count on their place in this

88 Macro- and Micropolitical Insurgency

scene, and who always counted on the possibility of reprising their role whenever they wished to do so) respond differently when faced with the anguish that the destabilization of this scene causes in them. If the politics of desire that guides their response is an active one – this is more and more common, albeit still not frequent enough – this experience can thrust them into the same movement that made the women characters transmute themselves. What follows is an overcoming both of men's disconnection with the extrapersonal and of the impossibility to sustain themselves in the tension between the personal and the extrapersonal. Men can then be guided by the effects of the destabilization on their bodies. With the activation of their body-knowing, men, too, can re-create themselves (guided by the affects) in their interactions with the new characters composed by the women with whom they share the scene, becoming, like them, agents of micropolitical insurgency.

When this happens, the new characters composed of women will, on their part, tend to transmute – and will continue to transmute – based on the affects resulting from the new dynamics of interaction. New dances, new choreographies are thus created. Through them, new scripts can emerge, where the politics of desire that orients both these characters and the dynamic of their relation is no longer subject to the pimp-colonial-capitalistic unconscious. This process will lead to the formation of a different regime of the unconscious and to the consequent establishment of new kinds of scenes in the social field, far removed from sexism.

Obviously, though, cancelling the theater of sexism and invalidating the male character in its role as oppressor can also lead this character to a reactive, violent response, one moved by its exasperated wish to conserve the scene and its characters just as they are, at any cost, for fear of collapsing. Unfortunately, this tendency has not only been prevalent; it has, in fact, expanded exponentially in recent times. One of its most obvious manifestations is the atrocious increase in the number of femicides, which take place just as feminist movements advance everywhere, especially in former colonies, in places such as Latin America and Africa. The growing strength of feminism is, moreover, one of the events that triggered the tsunami of conservatism (more and more narrow-minded and cruel) that has devastated the planet.

Macro- and Micropolitical Insurgency   89

In sum, there is a fundamental difference between macro- and micropolitical struggles in terms of their respective approaches to power relations. While the macropolitical operation of resistance seeks to redistribute places inside the web of power relations, the insurrectional operation corresponding to the sphere of micropolitics seeks to act differently, in a way that dismantles these relations, dissolving its characters, their respective roles, and their whole scene. To fight against the pimping of the drive (the marrow of the colonial-capitalist unconscious) implies constructing for oneself a different body. It implies molting out of an outgrown shell structured in a dynamic of abuse, the same way grasshoppers molt out of their exoskeletons so that another body, still embryonic, can fully flourish and take its place. And if this struggle takes place by affirmation and not by opposition (as is the case in macropolitics), this is because the dynamics of tension between the personal and the extrapersonal are not, in this case, dialectical but, rather, paradoxical. Confronting this tension entails affirmative actions of a becoming-other of the characters involved in the scene of power relations.

In this operation of micropolitical struggle, the borders between politics, the clinic, and art become indiscernible. The clinical dimension of this struggle rests in the fact that its objective is to free the unconscious from its colonial-capitalistic yoke. It is an effort to *heal* life as much as possible from its impotence, which is an after-effect of its captivity in a relational weave of abuse that alienates subjectivity from the demands of the drive and that keeps desire captive in the dominant regime, submissive in the face of this regime's pimping essence. And if this therapeutic operation is inseparable from an artistic operation, this is because healing in the sense invoked here can only be completed with the creation of new modes of existence. These modes materialize vital demands, thus completing the germination of the embryonic worlds that beat inside each body. Ultimately, every gesture of micropolitical insurrection is a movement towards the resurrection of life. It is a movement of that very resurrection.

If I use the term "artistic operation" to refer to the creation of new modes of existence that can embody vital demands, this is because in modern, Western culture (a culture that corresponds to the colonial-capitalistic regime), creation as a force is restricted to that specific activity conventionally referred to as "art," institutionalized as such just over two centuries ago. This being the case, the micropolitical mode of operating entails freeing the exercise of creation from its confinement in the field of art to the fullest extent possible, so that it can be reactivated in other practices of social life and in artistic practices themselves, because under financialized capitalism it became close to impossible to exercise creation even in the field of art. This is because art, under the new fold of the regime, became a privileged site for the pimping of the vital potency of creation.

Given the grip colonial-capitalistic abuse has on all of us (no one, not even the artist, escapes this grip), we're now at a point where ensuring that the force of creation remains channeled towards its ethical destiny has become notoriously challenging, even in the sphere of art. The specificity of this abuse in the field of art consists not just in neutralizing the potency of creation and reducing it to creativity but also in using it as an ostentatiously displayed access badge for entry into the international elites. To be a collector, to know the name of half a dozen artists and curators (the hottest ones on the market), to be a frequent guest at art openings and art fairs, and to tour and sightsee around the great art exhibitions of the world: all this has now become an essential element of the glamor projected onto the sterile existence of the elites, a glamor that imbues them with an air of seduction and that increases the value of their self-brand on the market. Furthermore, beyond the micropolitical advantages (i.e., increasing their narcissistic capital) that art brings to the elites, and beyond the effects this has on their macropolitical power (i.e., increasing their economic capital), art brings to them an added economic advantage: art has become, more than ever, a privileged site for speculation and money laundering.

7) Modes of Cooperation

Macropolitics (via identitarian recognition, so as to build organized movements and/or political parties)
Cooperation in a macropolitical insurrection functions through the construction of organized movements and/or political parties. The agents of this mode of insurrection are grouped via *identitarian recognition*. This is a pragmatic effort, made on the basis of a previously outlined action plan, and with an eye towards a goal linked to the same claim (which, in this macropolitical

sphere, is a concrete demand) and as a function of the same (subaltern) position within a determined segment of social life. It is through this position (which is located on the personal side of subjective experience) that an imagined identitarian outline is drawn, which creates a connection with others and provides the necessary basis for group formation on the grounds of identification.

Several segments of social life can come together in this way, around claims that involve, for instance, gender, race, and class. Movements, too, can come together around a single cause that concerns several of them. This is a mode of cooperation that generates momentum towards an effective reversal of power relations in the institutional sphere (which includes the state and its laws, but which cannot be reduced to it). The time of that struggle in each one of these movements is chronological, and it ends when its objective is reached. The movement, however, remains organized in order to face other emerging targets.

Micropolitics (via resonating frequencies of the affects, and towards the construction of the common)[43]

Cooperation within micropolitical insurrection takes place through the construction of the common. The agents of this insurrection find each other and grow close to each other by means of the *intensive resonance*[44] that manifests between the frequencies of affects (between vital emotions). These agents find and grow close to each other by weaving multiple, connecting webs between subjectivities and groups that are living through different situations, with singular languages and experiences, but united by a common element: the embryonic futures, the seeds that inhabit all the bodies involved in those webs. These seeds impose on agents the urgency to create forms that can materialize those worlds, thus completing their process of germination. This is only possible in a relational field, so long as desires guided by an ethical compass prevail in this field. When this happens, the result is that the actions driven by these desires are necessarily singular. The results, then, are different modes of expression of these embryonic futures, which interact and together create the ground for their own birth and generate new formations in the social field.

Temporary, relational territories thus emerge, varied and variable. Collective synergies are produced in these territories,

92 Macro- and Micropolitical Insurgency

synergies that nurture a reciprocal kind of reception that promotes, values, and legitimizes daring experimentation processes involving modes of existence that differ from hegemonic ones. These collective experiences expand the possibility of working through the trauma brought about by the perverse operation of the colonial-capitalistic regime, which restricts subjectivities to dominant forms and values marked by the expropriation of the creating potency of the drive.[45] Because working through this trauma is an endless task, what matters here is that this task reaches, in every situation, a threshold that allows for the vital drive to flow freely: freely enough, at least, to break away from its pimping. This is the condition necessary for the composition of an individual and a collective body that can resist the pimping of life and that can rebuff this pimping. The meaning of the term "the common" as proposed here consists precisely in this: the composition of this kind of collective body.

The possibility of constituting fields favorable for the emergence of an "event" – which is to say, the emergence of an effective transfiguration in the fabric of society – hinges upon these kinds of collective reappropriations of the drive. Thus conceived, an event is the result of the germination of embryonic worlds that resonate across bodies and lead those bodies to unite, producing a birthing nest for other modes of existence and for their respective cartographies.

In sum, the modes of cooperation proper to macro- and micropolitical insurrection are completely different, but they are complementary and indispensable, as are all the other aspects of macro- and micropolitical insurrections. Events – transfigurations of the established – are the result of creating processes proper to micropolitical insurgency; they differ from macropolitical insurrectional actions, which unfold according to a predefined and already resolved form. While the macropolitical mode of cooperation generates pressure that makes possible a *more equitable distribution of rights* in the present cartography, the micropolitical mode of cooperation generates a force of *transindividual metamorphosis*[46] that creates new cartographies where the right to life can be fulfilled.

Moreover, to come together through "resonance" is different than to gather by means of "identification." Both kinds of links are important. The problem comes when subjectivity confines itself within identitarian boundaries, reducing itself to them. This reduction tends to interrupt the processes of subjectivation set off by the tension between the personal and the extrapersonal: the tension produced in subjectivity by the effects of the forces of the other at the micropolitical level, if and when these effects manage to go beyond identitarian boundaries, in a way that threatens to dissolve them. Once these processes are interrupted, there is no chance for an effective transformation of reality, for there won't be any metamorphoses of the politics of subjectivation and of the new modes of existence that would be created as a result of these politics.

Decolonizing the Unconscious is the Matrix of Micropolitical Insurrection

In light of the new state of affairs, we cannot postpone combining the programmatic protest of consciousnesses with the drive-protest of the unconsciousnesses. As this essay has insistently stated, the disarticulation between the two spheres of struggle (the macro- and micropolitical) only adds to the infinite reproduction of the status quo. Worse still is the establishment of a conflictive polarity between macro- and micropolitical insurgency agents, a mutual demonization anchored on clashing views of what a supposedly "true revolutionary action" should be. This kind of relationship, which was unfortunately much too common in the revolts of the 1960s and 1970s, brought about several misunderstandings, causing unease in their agents and the depotentialization of the movement, especially on the micropolitical side. The fact is that both "revolution" and "truth" are concepts created in the realm of the politics of the production of an anthropo-phallo-ego-logocentric subjectivity proper to modern, Western, pimp-colonial-capitalistic culture. Our task is, therefore, to overcome in ourselves the nefarious dichotomy between micro- and macropolitics, looking for ways to articulate them in every relational field, in our everyday, and in collective insurrectional movements.

To complete this task, we must, first and foremost, refine our diagnosis of the hegemonic regime of the unconscious and of its toxic effects on both individual and collective existence, and we must do so from an ethical perspective. This refinement depends on the inextricability of a transdisciplinary theoretical inquiry, on the one hand, and a clinical-aesthetic-political pragmatics, on the other. The goal is to create conceptual-pragmatic instruments useful in the decolonization of the unconscious, the target of micropolitical insurrection. And if this task is imposed on us today with unprecedented urgency, this is because the struggle in that sphere is still in its infancy; it started to insinuate itself more widely only a little more than a half a century ago, since the 1950s, after World War II. The somber experience of that sad episode in history brought to us the intuition that it is not enough to rise up macropolitically, because micropolitical reactivity can reach extremely high levels of violence against life: genocides involving millions of persons with unimaginable refinements of perversion.[47] But still, it was only two decades later (in the 1960s and 1970s, with the rise of a postwar generation) that a micropolitical movement hatched, storming the whole fabric of society in several regions of the planet. The experience of insurrection in the micropolitical sphere is, therefore, much more recent than the insurrections that have taken place in the macropolitical sphere, which date back more than a century and half ago, to the time of the Paris Commune in 1871. The amount of experiences we have linked to insurrection in this sphere is thus much larger.

The decolonization of the unconscious involves subtle and complex work from all of us, work which stops only with death. Decolonization is never completed once and for all. But every time we manage to take a step further in that direction, it means we have one particle fewer of the dominant regime in us and around us. And each dissolution of a particle of that regime carries the power to propagate, dissolving other particles of the regime lodged in the social body. It is in these moments that life takes a leap, bringing us the individual and collective joy of its transfiguring affirmation. To desire this event – the event of a life that is not pimped – is the antidote for the pathology of the colonial-capitalistic regime, the one that makes life generic, the one that makes us crave the jouissance of power. This is a jouissance proper to a subjectivity reduced to the subject. It is a visionless jouissance, its heedlessness leading us to miserable and devastating forms of narcissism.

The New Modality of Coup
A Series in Three Seasons

A sinister landscape took hold of our planet after the globalitarian rise to power of the new, financialized, and neoliberal fold of the capitalist regime. It is carrying the regime's colonial project to its full, globalitarian realization. At the same time, another phenomenon has been adding toxicity to the atmosphere of this present landscape. Conservative forces are on the rise everywhere, with a degree of violence and barbarity that brings to mind, among other examples (from the twentieth century alone), the years of fascism, Nazism, and Stalinism in Europe, and the dictatorships in South America. It seems these conservative forces never actually disappeared, that they merely made a strategic and temporary retreat, lurking about in search of favorable conditions for their triumphal return.

Neoliberals and Neoconservatives United? Really?

At first sight, the simultaneous nature of these two phenomena (a new fold of capitalism; the reemergence of conservative forces) seems paradoxical. Though they both emanate from reactive forces, they are radically distinct, as different as their respective historical contexts. Beyond the more obvious differences (the transnationalism of globalitarian capitalism and the nationalism of neoconservative forces, for instance), the high degree of complexity, flexibility, sophistication, and perverse refinement of the neoliberal mode of existence and its strategies of power are light years ahead of the narrow-minded archaism and rigidity of neoconservatism. Neoconservatism, in fact, is only "new" to the extent that it hinges upon historical conditions different from those of its previous versions. Neoconservatism, in other words, is not a new conservatism; it is a return of conservatism or, more precisely, of a conservatism of the most brutish kind.

Even though the coexistence of these two regimes and their collusion can muddle our comprehension, once we get past our initial perplexity, it becomes evident that the neoliberal fold of capitalism needs to have neoconservative subjects temporarily in power. They act as goons who do the dirty work necessary for the establishment of a state in the service of transnational financial circuits. The intended result of this dirty work is the production of a twisted version of concepts associated with democratic and republican traditions. This brings about a veritable semantic chaos, which muddles the very memory of everything achieved by such traditions. The cognitive short-circuit produced by this chaos lines up perfectly with the mental patterns of these henchmen, and this, in turn, allows them to complete their task deftly and more efficiently. There is a micropolitical strategy at work here, and it is on the basis of this strategy that neoconservative subjects (working at the behest of financialized capitalism) will execute their second task. The purpose of this task points to the macropolitical sphere. It consists in undermining every democratic and republican achievement at the level of state structures. Along with that, it seeks to eliminate all politicians (especially leftist ones) identified with these achievements.

Shared interests around precisely this last goal paves the way for the temporary alliance between neoconservative and neoliberal forces. The clumsy subjectivity of neoconservatives is explicitly and fervently classist, racist, and macho (it also has colonial, slavocrat, and patriarchal undertones). This allows them to play their part without ethical or moral boundaries and with dizzying speed, and we can see how this plays out in the legislative branch. In the case of Brazil, by the time we recognize a legislative attack by neoconservatives, more attacks are already on their way, facilitated, for the most part, by representative bodies meeting in the middle of the night, under the cloak of

The New Modality of Coup 97

darkness. The fact that this work is handsomely rewarded by the executive office makes it more appealing for Brazilian neoconservative legislators. In exchange for this dirty work, they receive absurd amounts of public money for senseless projects tagged for their respective districts, which in turn helps these legislators in their efforts to please and broaden their local electoral base. Moreover, it is not uncommon for such legislators to also line their pockets from kickback schemes arranged with the private companies that receive the contracts for these projects. Aside from the fact that many of these contracts are established through rigged public bidding, the funding source for the bribes is often, of course, the overbilling for these same projects, which is another way of saying that the bribes are paid with money stolen from the public coffers.

Under these circumstances, room for negotiation opens up between the executive and the legislative branches of government. Lawmakers have the higher hand and they can blackmail the executive, demanding more and more money in return for their henchman work. Performing this task brings legislators a kind of perverse, narcissistic jouissance, unscrupulous to the point of obscenity. Pathetically, these lawmakers parade around full of conceit, proud of their self-image as violent machos capable of taking back power, the same power they held in the past, which was taken away from them by the rise of progressive forces in the years following the end of dictatorships. Little do they know that their dirty work prepares the ground for the advancement and the continuous strengthening of the hegemony of globalized circuits of capital and finance (which includes their local partners[48]), which will promptly dismiss them as soon as their work is no longer necessary. This is how the new kind of coup gets staged, the kind introduced by the current version of capitalism.

To better describe the nature of this kind of coup, the image that comes to my mind is that of a TV series, developed over three seasons. What brings this image to my mind is the fact that, day after day, the tactics of the coup, which is still ongoing, are transmitted on TV: in national news broadcasts that enjoy the highest ratings in Brazil, reaching almost all its regions. These newscasts are edited in way that creates a fictional, deceptive, and demonizing narrative of facts and their protagonists. They are televised to the whole of society with an aura of truth, with the aura of a news program that is supposed to be

98 The New Modality of Coup

impartial. What is more, such broadcasts mobilize a collective, TV-watching ritual performed by most Brazilian families, every day at the same time. When you also consider that each episode in the series is immediately discussed via social media, you realize that the series' plot lines spread exponentially, adapted to the cultural languages of the different social sectors that make up the audience of the news. This reinforces the credibility of the narrated events. These fictional narratives, together with both the collective ritual that they mobilize and the continuation of this ritual in social media, participate in the very micropolitical construction of the coup. Through this construction, the plot is imposed on the imaginary of Brazilians, preparing the ground for the execution of the macropolitical plan behind this new modality of coup.

The TV series (we can call it "The Coup") is produced in several Latin American countries, in different versions, adapted to each national context. The version I describe here is the Brazilian one; its script is thus based on events that took place in Brazil. Nevertheless, its plot, as well as the events on which it is based, tends to be equivalent in its adaptations in other countries on the continent. This is another way of saying that the strategy of the new modality of coup tends to be similar in all of them. It is likely that adaptations of the series are also actively disseminated in other countries: the US (under Trump), Poland, Hungary, Austria, Russia. This hypothesis, however, should be tested out by researchers with expertise in these national contexts.

In Latin America, the origin of the script dates back to the years after the end of dictatorships, when left-wing candidates began to win presidential elections[49] thanks in large part to the support of pro-democracy social movements. The first time any of these series featured an episode based on the impeachment of a president was in Paraguay in 2012. In this first version, the episode featuring the impeachment of President Fernando Lugo[50] comes early in the series. That this episode can be read as an episode belonging to a coup is evident, to the extent that coups are traditionally associated with the removal of presidents. But this should not lead us to think that the series we're calling "The Coup" begins or ends with this kind of episode: the new modality of coup seeks much more than the removal of presidents. In order to visualize the entire script of these series, I will focus on the Brazilian version.

The Script of the Series

The first season of the Brazilian version of this series began in 2004, with a bombastic image broadcasted in *Jornal Nacional*. It announced the news of arraignments related to a bribery scheme linked to representatives affiliated to the governing alliance of President Luiz Inácio da Silva (Lula). The scheme involved payouts made in exchange for budgetary and legislative support for development projects proposed by the executive branch of the Lula administration. Because of the monthly nature of this scheme, it became known as the "Mensalão" (the "big monthly payment"). The episode brings together footage of the TV anchors announcing this news with images of thousands of Brazilian families in front of their TV sets, astonished by the news. The following episode centers on the 2005 establishment in Congress of the Comissão Parlamentar Mista de Inquérito (CPMI), a joint parliamentary committee charged with investigating the bribery scheme. The objective of this committee was to investigate accusations against members of the Partido dos Trabalhadores (PT, Workers' Party) and members of the other parties that joined the governing alliance of Lula's presidency.

The Brazilian version of the first season of the series continued into 2006, with accusations made against thirty-eight government agents involved in the bribery scheme. Charges were brought in the highest court in Brazil, the Supreme Federal Court (Supremo Tribunal Federal, STF), with Chief Justice Joaquim Barbosa as its rapporteur. A later chapter in the series focused on Chief Justice Barbosa, who started criminal proceedings against the accused in 2007. It also shed light on two figures chosen (out of the thirty-eight accused) by the media as the principal protagonists of the bribery scheme: José Dirceu, the former minister of the Casa Civil (a position more or less comparable to that of chief of staff, which made him the most powerful member of President Lula's cabinet), and José Genoíno, who was at the time president of the Workers' Party. Images of these new events kept appearing, interwoven with images of the faces of thousands of increasingly enraged Brazilian citizens. Some of these citizens appeared on TV commenting on all this as they watch it daily unfolding on their own TV screens.

100 The New Modality of Coup

In a later chapter, still in the first season, we see the massive protests that shook Brazil in June 2013, which went on for months (later episodes in the series did not include coverage of these protests). What led masses of people onto the streets was both macro- and micropolitical in nature. The macropolitical reason for the protests was indignation created by the news of corruption of the Workers' Party government, news broadcast by the series that had already been on TV for a year. Among the more progressive sectors, this added to a chorus of existing outcries regarding both spurious political alliances established by the government of the Workers' Party and excessive government spending related to Brazil's planning for the World Cup and the Olympic Games. Businesses involved in the planning of these events and linked to the kickback scheme mentioned above overbilled the government for their services at a time when a number of public services were faltering due to underinvestment. The micropolitical reason for these protests is less obvious but perhaps more fundamental. It resides in the malaise that the series managed to cause in Brazilian society, which generated a mixture of entangled responses ranging from the most active to the most reactive.

The uprising of social segments moved by the more active forces came as a response to the lack of consideration the Workers' Party showed towards the micropolitical demands of these same social segments. It also came as a response to the micropolitical strategy of the series. Even though its script is based on actual instances of corruption, what enraged these social segments was both the way the series distorted facts and the way these distortions were used to manipulate subjectivities. This added to the ever expanding and ever more brutal proliferation of fake news in social media.

The uprising of those segments of the population that were moved by more reactive forces was a response that had already been contemplated by the micropolitical strategy of the coup. The focus of the rage that fueled these forces was the Workers' Party and the left in general, both portrayed as if they were the only political entities guilty of corruption. This is precisely what the strategy behind the series sought to bring about, and this made manifest the latent hatred that elites and middle-class segments of the population had for the Workers' Party and its leadership: a class hatred against Lula (given his *nordestino* and

The New Modality of Coup 101

working-class roots); a hatred corresponding to the colonial and slavocrat tradition that impregnates the subjectivity of these social sectors; and a hatred that gained credibility and legitimacy thanks to the strategy of the coup. But the mobilization of these forces did not stop there. Hatred against Lula and the Workers' Party expanded and grew more and more intense in the following seasons of the series, eventually reaching voters from the popular segments of the population that had previously supported Lula.

In the immediate aftermath of these protests, the pace of the series began to accelerate, in clear response to the social uprisings that took place in Brazil in 2013. Five months after those uprisings took place, a new episode was released, featuring the sentencing by Chief Justice Barbosa (who by that time had been named the president of the Federal Supreme Court) of twenty of the accused in the case of the *Mensalão*. Ten of these defendants (among them the two key Workers' Party figures mentioned above: José Dirceu and José Genuino) went to prison on November 15, 2013, the day of the anniversary of the Proclamation of the Republic. This was not a mere coincidence. The series used, micropolitically, the image of the two leaders of the Workers' Party going to prison as an emblem of the celebrations of an historical event. The intent behind this micropolitical strategy, in turn, was to lead us to believe that what we were witnessing was the restoration of republican ideals, which were supposedly destroyed by the governments of the Workers' Party. The whole operation was quite successful. It generated fervent, patriotic support for the coup from a significant part of the Brazilian population.

In the episode that follows, the same ploy was repeated. In 2014, Operation Car Wash (Operação Lava Jato) began.[51] It consisted of more than one thousand investigations by the Brazilian Federal Police, authorized by Sérgio Moro (then a federal judge) and intended as a probe into a money-laundering scheme that involved billions of Brazilian reais in bribes. The operation resulted in hundreds of people sent to prison. Twenty-three of the accused (business owners or executives of enterprises with links to Petrobrás, the national Brazilian oil company) also received prison sentences in 2014, once again on the Day of the Proclamation of the Republic, following the same micropolitical strategy used the previous year.

102 The New Modality of Coup

Facing all of this, Brazilians less prone to manipulation were already sensing that what had really been commemorated for two years in a row on the anniversary of the Proclamation of the Republic was the triumphal return of the Banana Republic. This was the style of government that characterized the Brazilian republic since its founding, interrupted only briefly during the years when the Workers' Party was in power, when dreams of a New Republic appeared to be actually materializing. In its recent incarnation, the Banana Republic style of government can come across as retro or old-fashioned, to the extent that it evokes a colonial and slave-holding tradition. But what the return of that style really reveals is that the visceral presence of the colonial and slave-holding tradition in Brazil never ceased to exist in the subjectivity of its middle and elite classes. Not only did that tradition make a return; it was both brashly paraded and barely disguised in the script of the new coup as a supposed return to democracy. This constitutes yet another micropolitical effect of the new modality of the coup.

In the first part of the series, one of the climax points in the plot line is the moment when the Supreme Federal Court of Brazil assumes a starring role. For the first time in the history of this institution, created at the end of the nineteenth century, the Supreme Federal Court sent politicians to prison. Strangely enough, despite the fact that the scheme of the so-called *mensalão* scandal was adopted by all the administrations that preceded those of the Workers' Party (with exorbitant bribes exchanged through various procedures and not necessarily distributed on a monthly basis), no politician had ever been tried for this kind of crime before, much less sentenced to prison. Corruption, of course, must be opposed, but, when we take all the preceding facts into consideration, we realize that from the outset anti-corruption proceedings were pursued not for the sake of fighting corruption but, rather, as part of the operation of the coup. This was made possible thanks to an alliance between judicial and police forces, large media corporations (which broadcast and disseminate events related to the coup), and transnational, financialized capital.

Early on in the new coup, it became clear that, in the series' script, politics and the judicial branch of government were wholly aligned. This alignment itself was not a new development in Brazil. The judges involved in the operation of the

The New Modality of Coup   *103*

coup brashly manipulated and continue to manipulate extant constitutional law in favor of political interests that go hand in hand with economic interests. If necessary, they even change the constitution with jet-like speed. The politicians imprisoned for corruption, the standout characters in this episode of the coup, not only share in these political and economic interests; they also play a central role in the defense of the same interests. They are sentenced to prison despite the lack of concrete evidence against them (as was the case of Lula in the second season of the series). Meanwhile, others whose crimes have been scandalously proven are exonerated or receive much lighter sentences. In all these cases, there is absolutely no chance of predicting what the sentencing guidelines will be or how they will conform to current statutes. What does become possible is the identification of the political interests guiding punishment or exoneration in each criminal proceeding against corruption. There is not, however, any certainty about the strategies that will be used to justify these sentences.

Lifted by that alliance, and holding a majority in congress, the henchmen of the globalized circuits of capital and finance orchestrate the blow that takes down the more left-leaning government leaders. To demonize these leaders, they use, micropolitically, accusations of corruption (some of which are unproven) such as those mentioned above (this is what happened to Lula). They also make these leaders responsible for any economic crisis that the nation faces (as was the case with Dilma Rouseff).[52] These crises, of course, are nothing other than the local symptom of a global predicament. But the coup did not end with the punishment of the leaders of the Workers' Party, nor did it end with the micropolitical destruction of the democratic imaginary, which culminated in the last episode of the first season of the series (the episode featuring the impeachment of Dilma Rousseff in August 2016).

Once that first part of the dirty work is concluded, and once the democratic imaginary is partially destroyed, a second season of the series begins. Although other people get to play the part of the prisoners over the course of the series (which is to say, although other people end up imprisoned, aside from the group in the first part of the coup), left-leaning leaders – especially those affiliated to the Workers' Party – continue to be cast as the demonized characters. Lula was constantly in the crosshairs of

104 The New Modality of Coup

these corruption proceedings. His demonization, a focus of the micropolitical strategy of the coup, is featured in every episode of this series until the end of the second season, when his farcical prosecution and the ban imposed on him prohibiting him from running for office are complete.

The Second Season

The second season of the series features the necessary dismantlement of the constitution. In order to prepare this process micropolitically, the script focuses both on the terrifying portrayal of a ghost – the ghost of economic crisis – and on an intensifying strategy of destruction of the progressive imaginary, which by this point has already been partially undone (by the events portrayed in the first season of the series). The dismantlement of the constitution takes places thanks to another round of dirty work completed by the henchmen behind this process. The first part consists of a blockage of public spending. An amendment to the constitution,[53] passed on December 2016, froze public spending in Brazil for twenty years, under the pretense of addressing the economic crisis. This block on spending impacts development subsidies as well as budgets set aside for social programs, especially those concerning education and health. On top of the laws passed during the governments of the Workers' Party – laws that extended access to quality health and education for the majority of the population – the coup also dismantled the public university through cuts to both education funds and funds intended for the promotion of research.

Another round of dirty work of this season of the series consists in a crude reform of labor that, in Brazil, will go beyond increasing the precarity of work. At its worst, this labor reform legalizes demeaning working conditions that, until recently, had been constitutionally defined as slave-like conditions and thus punishable by law. On that note, it's worth highlighting that the decision to legalize such working conditions is a recognition of the fact that those conditions persist to this day, and not just in rural settings. The working conditions of undocumented migrants employed in the fashion industry in Brazil is just one example of this. The labor reform also has an impact on education, to the extent that it affects

The New Modality of Coup

private universities. In fact, immediately after the passage of laws related to the labor reform, several such universities fired faculty members en masse, substituting instructors with others hired without benefits and with miserable salaries. And it didn't stop there. Thanks, in large part, to the increased precarity of working conditions for faculty members, these universities can decrease the cost of tuition, attracting more students and increasing their enrollments. This, in turn, helps them burnish their brand. Advertising campaigns tinged with populism get rolled out, emphasizing what is supposed to be an institutional commitment on the part of these universities to social and democratic agendas.

The third and fourth rounds in this wave of dirty works consist in outrageous social security and pensions reforms, on the one hand, and the privatization of state companies and resources, on the other (either the most profitable ones or the ones that can be made profitable through spurious arrangements that increase the number of top state companies subject to privatization). In many cases, public approval of these privatizations is secured by forcing companies into financial collapse and then returning to the fictional script of the coup, which attributes the collapse to the bad management, inefficiency, and corruption of the companies' executives and, by extension, to the government officials who appointed these executives. And when the henchmen of the coup don't have enough votes in Congress to pass an amendment or law necessary for the kind of dismantlement described here, the transnational agencies responsible for the most consequent among global financial indicators will quickly enter onto the scene. These agencies (Standard & Poor's and Moody's Corporation, for instance) are leaders in the assessment of the global capital market and thus in investment risk analysis. Their operation consists in devaluing or threatening to devalue Brazilian credit ratings, which offers powerful ammunition – the threat of national debt default – for the approval of changes to public policy that face resistance in Congress. This is happening in Brazil in relation to pension reforms, and it had already taken place in Europe, in places such as Portugal, Ireland, Greece and Spain, the eloquently monikered group of PIGS.

This is how the first elements of the *res publica* get destroyed, the first elements of a social democracy incipiently established

106   The New Modality of Coup

in Brazil, with ups and downs, by the progressive governments that rose to power a few years after the end of the dictatorship. These governments were guided by the wish to establish the rule of law, a regime that never actually materialized in Brazil or in the vast majority of South American countries. This is the reason why the protagonists of progressive administrations, especially those affiliated to the Workers' Party, are the targets for the new modality of the coup, whose ultimate aim is to conclude the series with the wholesale establishment of a neoliberal state, a nation wholly focused on the interests of transnational capital and of its partners chosen from local elites. In other words, the ultimate aim of this new modality of the coup is to facilitate as much as possible the circulation of investments in a way that creates conditions for the multiplication of investment capital, as fast as possible.

While these maneuvers run their course, the henchmen of globalitarian capitalism themselves will also be accused of corruption, thus preparing the ground for their dismissal, which takes place as soon as their work is completed. In the last season of the series, the new regime throws these conservative figures into the trash bin of history, without the slightest hesitation. This is one difference between the new modality of the coup and the previous modality of military coups. Even though the latter were also executed by conservative agents (the military, in this case) working under the orders of the ruling powers of capitalism (powers that, at the time, were mostly linked to the United States), in that earlier context, the regime needed a totalitarian state, and in order to establish one it required the continuous presence of conservatives in power.

At the same time, and still in this second season of the series, while the political henchmen working for globalitarian capitalism are being accused of corruption, similar charges are also brought against executives running large companies. Banks are excluded from this operation, and not only that: a significant portion of their debts to the government is forgiven at precisely this moment. The targets in Brazil for accusations of corruption are mostly large companies that operate as cartels and that monopolize the vast majority of public works construction, not just in Brazil but also in parts of Latin America and Africa (the parts of those continents previously identified by these companies as promising future markets).

The New Modality of Coup 107

But why turn these characters into villains? After all, the takeover of these companies (especially the large construction companies) by the financial sector was fully completed in the first years of the twenty-first century, after the administration of President Fernando Henrique Cardoso (1995–2003), when investment companies were created to bring in transnational financial capital to this sector.[54] And why would these characters get turned into villains, despite the fact that this would evidently result in more power for their credit subsidiaries, who subjected construction companies to the financializing logic of investment firms?[55]

The series demonstrates that an alliance with the executives running these companies is only of interest to globalitarian capitalism inasmuch as it needs their support, not just in the destruction of the imaginary of the left (and of the defense of democratic laws that this imaginary upholds) but also in backing up and reinforcing the idea that we are facing an imminent economic apocalypse. With their support, favorable conditions are created for privatizing state companies and for repealing laws linked to the social agenda, especially labor laws. The reason behind the haste with which Brazilian senior executives are turned into the new villains in the series is that the ground must be prepared to expand the power of transnational capitalism and cement its leadership of the market, not just in terms of private businesses (which are, for the most, already completely under its command) but also and especially in terms of state enterprises (the control of which will be completely realized once the right to privatization is completely instituted). With that double expulsion – of both politicians and business executives – and with a severe institutional and economic crisis already established in the country (a crisis accentuated by the freeze in public works spending), the ground will be completely ready for total and unobstructed control of investment by transnational capital.

In that second season of the series, fighting scenes between different mafias of sordid politicians and between politicians and the mafias formed by elegant businessmen are particularly important narrative devices. Immune from prosecution thanks to the testimony they provide against each other, they mutually destroy each other in front of a society that witnesses, every night, this grotesque spectacle on their TV screens. This spectacle

108 The New Modality of Coup

trends constantly on social media, and it is also on display in the daily newspapers read by some members of the middle and upper classes.

With this vast and uninterrupted broadcasting of the series, society's attention is thus channeled towards the horrifying images and narratives of fraudulent political and economic negotiations. These images and narratives are secretly intercepted in telephone calls, emails, recordings, and documents, either obtained as part of plea bargains or else discovered by police as they search through offices and private residences. The whole thing reads like a true psychopathology TV show, and an entertaining one at that, to the extent that it reminds us of the funniest of B movies and their hammy actors. The sad difference is that, in this case, the fictional narrative is based on real events. If these facts, on their own, are sufficient cause for complete indignation, their effect is even greater. Because they are edited in the same way that events in a TV series are edited, and because this framing happens with the intention of preparing the ground for a coup, these facts can act micropolitically on subjectivities. They can propagate insecurity and they can propagate the fear of collapse.

Disinformation as Power Device: What's New?

There is nothing new about the way capitalism is now using discourse manipulation (whether visual or verbal) or about the way it is now constructing narratives that demonize its enemies and hide the reality of the facts. These have long been some of the micropolitical strategies employed to justify and make viable its macropolitical projects. They were widely used early on by the colonial-capitalist regime. Take but one example: the example of catechism, a kind of precursor to the narrative of fake news. The catechism was framed as the word of God, unique and universal and transmitted by the Catholic Church, a kind of Globo news corporation of its time. It was disseminated by the Jesuits, the main "news anchors" for the Catholic Church. The strategy was refined with the advances in mass communication platforms developed in the nineteenth century in parallel with the industrial revolution. Aside from being one of the central devices in the production of subjectivities by capitalism in

The New Modality of Coup 109

the twentieth century, these strategies were widely used both by totalitarian regimes in Europe and in preparation for the coups d'état that took place in the 1960s and 1970s in Latin America. That said, the way in which this power device gets updated by these two versions of capitalism (the industrial version and the financialized version) is different. Each one uses conservatism in a different sense. And each one uses different technologies to construct and disseminate fake narratives.

The exponential advances in information and communication technology that have taken place since the end of the 1970s has not only made the micro- and macropolitical use of such technologies more subtle and more powerful; they have also been partly responsible for capitalism's rise to globalitarian power (capitalism in its new fold). The propaganda narratives formulated by industrial capitalism (which were also built and financed by an alliance between business interests and politicians) were blunt, transmitted first by radio and televison and in movie theaters, before the screening of feature films. More recent advances in digital technology have significantly refined the role played by communication and information as devices in the service of power. These advances also brought about a growing sophistication of languages and techniques of manipulation and publicity, as well as a multiplication of available media platforms and a global expansion of real-time networks of communication.[56] And while the spread of false information is not a novelty (it has long contributed to the composition of fictive narratives imposed on subjectivities), what remains true is that this device has been refined exponentially in the twenty-first century. Not only does fake news go viral, thanks, in large part, to the role played by bots in the dissemination of digital information; it also simulates its own legitimacy by means of countless "likes" instantaneously produced by these same bots, which gives fake posts the appearance of being widely accepted as truths, intensifying and propagating their deception.

Another difference between the use of communication technology by industrial capitalism on the one hand and by financialized capitalism on the other lies in both the respective triggers they use to produce fear and insecurity and their respective impetus for the mobilization of conservative fury in each one of their historical contexts. In the 1950s and 1960s, still in the era of industrial capitalism, the trigger was the ghost of

110   The New Modality of Coup

communism propagated during the Cold War. This was a threat backed by the revelation at that time of the totalitarian horrors of Stalinism, which were then associated with Nazism and fascism, whose traumatic effects were still infecting subjectivities. The ghost of communism was projected onto all kind of governments with democratizing tendencies (this was the case with the Jango administration in Brazil and the Allende administration in Chile); the effects of this projection on the masses, in turn, prepared the ground for the coups d'état of the 1960s and 1970s.

Later, in the 1990s, the experiences that came after the fall of dictatorships with the rise of leftist governments mobilized an expansive sense of identification among the most disenfranchised – and most numerous – segments of society. By then, it was no longer possible to associate these governments with communism as a threatening ghost, and it was even less feasible to associate them with the totalitarian version of communism. This association was already largely dissolved by such geopolitical shifts as the end of the Cold War, the fall of the Berlin Wall, and the dissolution of the Soviet Union.[57]

From the perspective of the financialized fold of capitalism, what needed to be dissolved was the identification of a growing segment of the population (in the aftermath of the fall of dictatorships) with the progressive governments that rose to power at the time. To accomplish this, narratives were constructed and disseminated to single out corruption as a tool in the demonization of the left. If accusations of corruption (and their populist appeal) have been and continue to be widely used by those in power to eliminate their enemies, such accusations against leftist leaders have an added advantage: the obliteration of their image of honesty and of a sincere commitment to social justice. These are the main virtues attributed to leftist politicians in the imaginary of those who identify with them, and this is precisely the distinguishing feature of these politicians (on the whole, politicians in places such as Brazil have been traditionally associated with both corruption and their contempt for social issues). In the narrative constructed up until that point, the populist use of the fight against corruption, now turned against leftist politicians, inverts the signal in a way that transforms so-called corruption hunters into beacons of honesty, justice, and democracy. Associating someone such as Lula with corruption has the intended effect of destroying the expectation that his class origins can guarantee his commitment to social justice. The notion that all politics are carved from the same stone adds deception to the feelings of insecurity and fear, generating a kind of apathy grounded in exhaustion.

The use of micropolitical strategies by the colonial-capitalistic regime to complete its macropolitical projects is not limited to propaganda. This is only one of the devices in its micropolitical modus operandi, which is much more expansive and much more complex, and which has been in operation, with different twists and variations, since the fifteenth century. This is one of the fundamental elements of the modality of power corresponding to this regime.

Micropolitical Principle of Colonial-Capitalistic Power: The Abuse of Life

The micropolitical strategy of colonial-capitalistic power consists in producing a politics of subjectivation that has as its goal the abuse of life as force of creation and mutation. This force is channeled away from its ethical destiny. The continuity of life itself, not just human life, depends on this destiny. In the case of humans, abuse is not restricted to the way that potency is manifested as labor force, as it was previously postulated by certain dominant strains of Marxism; it includes all the ways in which this potency is manifested. In order for this abuse to take place, the subject must be prevented from accessing this potency and the indispensable knowledge of the dynamics of this potency, a knowledge which should be developed throughout the course of a life to better protect life, and to direct it towards its ethical destiny. Preventing the subject from accessing this potency strips the subject from this knowledge, and so it strips it of the power to make choices aligned with whatever life demands from it. It turns the subject into a docile and submissive subject, relative to the modes of existence necessary for the colonial-capitalistic regime, which are based on the exploitation of subjectivity's vital potency.

In the most recent fold of the regime, interventions in the sphere of subjectivity have become more and more refined and more and more intense. The abuse of the vital force goes deeper and deeper. Its objective is no longer limited to making

112 The New Modality of Coup

the subject more docile and more submissive (this was the aim during the first and second industrial revolutions). On the contrary, the objective is now to stimulate that potency into accelerating and intensifying its productivity, all the while diverting it from its ethical destiny. The creating ability, intrinsic to this potency, gets dissociated from life and from the demands life makes for new modes of existence cultivated in response to the demands of life. Reduced to mere creativity, this potency can then be invested in the composition of new scenarios for the accumulation of capital (economic, political, cultural, and narcissistic capital).

Instead of the creation of the new, what is produced – "creatively" and more and more rapidly – are novelties, which multiply opportunities for the investment of capital and stimulate the desire to consume. And although the desire to consume was already mobilized by the previous fold of the regime, it now has at its disposal a continuous outburst of new products. Images of these new products reach subjectivity like bombs that detonate in every direction, dispersed incessantly by technologies of information and communication. They ceaselessly feed the desire to consume, transforming it into compulsive voraciousness. This is another way of saying that the vital potency, in its very essence, is twisted into the interests of reproducing the status quo, changing nothing but the "creative" placement of its pieces or substituting these pieces for other, interchangeable ones, infinitely reproducing variations of the same.

If the new kind of coup d'état has no recourse to military force, this is not just because rigid, totalitarian, and nationalist governments are not convenient to it. Beyond those macropolitical reasons, there are other, micropolitical ones. Rigid, identitarian subjectivities of the kind linked to industrial capitalism represent an inconvenience for the new regime. The previous capitalist regime needed docile bodies that remained sedentary; it needed everyone in their right place, organized and disciplined like factory workers. In contrast to that, financialized capitalism needs flexible and "creative" subjectivities that can mold themselves, both in production and in consumption, to the new scenarios that the regime produces incessantly. In other words, in its new fold, the regime needs subjectivities that have enough malleability to circulate through various places and functions, enough malleability to

The New Modality of Coup 113

transform their self-image and their habits in order to consume emerging new products. This allows them to keep up with the breakneck, continuous, and infinitesimal movement of capital and information.

This is yet another reason why the use of military force is of no interest to the new version of capitalism as it goes about orchestrating its coups. To execute these coups, the new version of capitalism proceeds micropolitically, relying on the force of desire. This is accomplished by means of the corruption of desire, which takes place at the same time that the henchmen of capitalism complete their brute work on the macropolitical sphere. That same, micropolitical reason explains the fact that financialized capitalism is not interested in keeping conservatives in power after the completion of the new modality of coups. This is because, as I argued above, the rigid, nationalist, authoritarian form of government embraced by these conservatives is not in the interest of financialized capitalism.

One unanticipated phenomenon is that flexible subjectivity as it developed over the course of the 1980s and 1990s, just as financialized capitalism was becoming established at a globalitarian level, ended up generating, at the end of the 1990s, a hatching of collective movements that deflected the power that the pimp-colonial-capitalistic unconscious held over the choices made and the actions taken by subjects. Faced with this phenomenon, the regime implemented another operation. In order to describe this operation, let's return to the image of the TV series that constitutes the coup.

The Conservative Tantrum

Towards the end of the second season of the series, once the manipulation of subjectivities is well underway, another power device comes into scene, one that will have a more direct and vehement impact on the micropolitical sphere and that will also be deployed macropolitically, in an instrumental way. The rude henchmen of neoliberalism are called upon to deploy this device, perfect as they are for this task given their vile state of mind and their anxious will to massacre anyone who does not reflect their sense of self. What takes place towards the end of the second season of the series, then, is an increase in the violence of the

114 The New Modality of Coup

conservative tantrum, which spreads more and more throughout the social body.

Church-based "family values" and identitarian morals are fanatically invoked during this moment, "values" and morals that were present since the first episodes of the series but that now come to the fore with delirious insistence. Culture in its widest sense – artistic, educational, therapeutic, and non-Christian religious practices, as well as every mode of existence that does not fit into sexist, aggressively masculine, heteronormative, homophobic, transphobic, racist, classist, and xenophobic categories – is turned into a target. These modes of existence are the ones usually tagged as "minorities," not in a quantitative sense but in the sense of their classification as qualitatively inferior, from the point of view of the hegemonic mode of existence. These so-called minoritarian modes of existence do not fit into the pattern that disconnects subjects from what life demands from them. They are classified as inferior because their modes of existence are singular. In this sense, we can accurately refer to these "minorities" as minoritized majorities, given that the ability to go beyond the dominant mode of subjectivation is potentially present in the majority of subjects.[58]

Widely denounced in the media, certain practices come to be perceived as demonic, just as they were during the times of the Inquisition, when certain practices by women (practices guided by the knowledge proper to living beings) were pejoratively flagged as "witchcraft," a name that justified their imprisonment, torture, and killing (more than a million women accused of being witches have been killed to date).[59] Demonization as a device for the manipulation of subjectivities prepares the ground for legislative changes that affect the subjects most liable to demonization: changes to women's rights, reproductive rights, sexual rights, etc. Let's focus on three examples, all of which unfolded in Brazil in the second half of 2017.

The first example is art. Certain artistic practices, especially those that have anything to do with matters related to gender, sexuality or religion, get disqualified, persecuted, and criminalized. Two birds get killed with one stone: practices linked to modes of being that do not fit into the dominant forms are demonized; by extension, the ethical dignity of art (in its active exercise of the creating drive) is also demonized, thereby neutralizing its micropolitical potency. By micropolitical potency

The New Modality of Coup 115

I mean art's potency to make life's demands (the demands life makes whenever it sees itself suffocated by current forms of individual and collective existence) sensible, perceptible by feeling. Materialized in art works, these vital demands have the capacity to pollinate the publics that have access to them, which then tends to mobilize a collective force of transfiguration (of forms of reality) and transvaloration (of reality's values). In this sense, attacks on art constitute attacks on the possibility of the social irruption of this force, which makes its reappropriation by subjects even more difficult.

The second example concerns movements (feminist movements, LGBTQ+ movements, trans movements, etc.) that bring about mutations in subjectivities and, inseparably, in their modes of existence, especially in the realms of sexuality and of gender relations. The operation in this case consists in mobilizing for a return to monogamous, hetero-cis-normative values, the values of the patriarchal nuclear family, the supposed universal form for social bonds and for eroticism (an eroticism that, in this case, is the result of low vital potency). The objective here is to interrupt the drive-process behind the creation of new modes of existence in the realms of sexuality and of gender relations. This is a process that tends to unleash and propagate as a response to life's urgent need to recover its potency in these realms, realms whose forms weaken the potency of life.

The third example relates to indigenous peoples and Afro-descendants who, together, tend to constitute the majority in ex-colonial societies.[60] In those societies, the dominant attitude towards such segments of the population is founded on humiliation and stigmatization of their modes of existence. This extends to the reception of and, most importantly, the perspective that guides their cultural traditions. These are traditions that incarnate in new forms of existence, as a response to the effects of new social, animal, plant, and cosmic ecologies. Humiliation and stigmatization of such traditions is nothing new. What's different now is that these traditions and the second-class citizens who practice them are openly and abjectly disqualified by those in power, proudly and without the slightest hint of shame, in line with what's taken to be a universal truth.

In Brazil, the intensification of this violence in the period we're here discussing is evident in the case of Afro-descendants. We can see this, for instance, in the increasing number of murders among

116   The New Modality of Coup

black youth and in systemic attacks against Candomblé[61] meeting places (*terreiros*). Associating this Afro-religious practice with the devil justifies its destruction. Attackers tend to be fundamentalist evangelicals who divulge their hatred and destruction of Afro-religions openly, bragging about their violence in the media and on social networks. This violence is also manifest when it targets indigenous communities, whose ancestral lands are constantly stolen despite the inextricable, visceral link between such lands and the cultural traditions of these communities (to say nothing of the obvious importance of the lands as sources of food, the production of which is inseparably linked to cultural tradition in many indigenous communities). The takeover of indigenous lands has been occurring nonstop since the early days of colonization. In the present day, the difference is that laws enacted to protect lands designated as indigenous lands, either ancestral lands under continuous indigenous occupation or lands granted following the displacement of indigenous peoples in the past, are now abolished. These are laws enacted as part of the Brazilian Constitution of 1988, the result of a long and arduous struggle that unfolded over the course of several decades. Today, the expulsion of indigenous people from their lands takes place with the support of stakeholders in agrobusiness and in the lumber and mining industries. In most cases, here as elsewhere, the first step in this process is the assassination of indigenous leaders, which sets up the conditions necessary for the removal of whole communities or, if necessary, their genocide and the destruction of their villages.

The third example of micropolitical operations (in this case, in the realm of Afro-descendant and indigenous traditions) prepares the ground for legislative changes. The objective of these operations is more obviously macropolitical: to expropriate Candomblé meeting places and indigenous lands, and to neutralize black and indigenous movements that have recently gained strength.[62] If we compare this example of a micropolitical operation with the other two operations taking place (in the field of art and in regard to minorities), it is evident that micropolitical operations create conditions for legislative changes related to the social and the environmental agenda in the sphere of macropolitics.

In the health sector in Brazil, federal representatives have been working to revive a legislative initiative that would classify homosexuality as a disease, subject to treatment. Implementing this law would justify and legalize so-called conversion therapies, whether religious or psychological. The goal of these "therapies" is to transform and "normalize" the sexual orientation of all those whose practices differ from the dominant categories of gender and sexuality. It's worth remembering that, since the 1990s, the World Health Organization (WHO) has disregarded any project under its consideration that rests on the premise of homosexuality as a disease. It's also worth remembering that, in Brazil, the Federal Council of Psychology (Conselho Federal de Psicologia) advised against this link in 1999, in line with recommendations previously made by the Federal Council of Medicine (Conselho Federal de Medicina).

It is, at the very least, surprising, even startling, that this specter of sorts was revived in Brazil precisely in 2017, rekindling a heated polemic. But the return of this phantasm will seem less surprising if we position ourselves in the universe of micropolitical operations that form part of the script of the coup. Considered from this perspective, the fact that this legislative project was not approved does not obstruct its impact as a micropolitical power device that impacts the production of subjectivity. Micropolitical insubordination in the fields of sexuality and erotic-affective relationships have once again been turned into scapegoats in the eyes of those subjectivities more completely dominated by the regime of the colonial-capitalistic unconscious, who project their own malaise onto those who commit insurrection in this field. The homophobias, transphobias, machismos, and toxic masculinities that have always been expressed without fear of punishment in Brazilian society started to reemerge with renewed violence, explicitly and shamelessly.

In the field of education, discussions in Congress related to the new Brazilian National Common Core Curriculum (Base Nacional Comum Curricular, BNCC) demonized the inclusion of any content related to politics (in the spirit of "Escola sem partido," as the slogan in Portuguese goes), as well as so-called gender identity, sexual orientation, or Afro-descendant and indigenous cultures. The new national curriculum approved in 2017 eliminated passages from previous versions that stressed the need for an education free of prejudices. More specifically, more than ten passages that mentioned matters related to gender and sexuality were excluded, and books on Orixá mythology, given their allegedly "demonic" content, were eliminated from the bibliography. These cuts in the national school curriculum are ballasted by the micropolitical operations mentioned above, the ones targeting LGBTQI+, Afro-descendants, and indigenous peoples and cultures. They form part of the same social narrative that now has a new character in its cast of villains.

The same micropolitical aspect of power operations in the macropolitical sphere can also be found in budget cuts affecting public universities and their research initiatives. Historically, access to public universities has been a privilege for the wealthiest segments of Brazilian society, and this fact began to change during the administrations of the Workers' Party. The dismantlement of the public university system thus indicates that the education coup has an impact beyond the level of access to education available to the vast majority of the population. Its micropolitical objective is to reduce access to information and to intellectual formation in Brazil (this does not affect members of the elite, who still have access to foreign, private, well-regarded universities). The result of this is a further weakening of the potency of thought, as well as a decrease in the ability to decipher what it is that asphyxiates life in the present, an ability that can free life through the creation of new scenarios.

The micropolitical dimension of the education coup also includes the effects of the new labor law on private universities. The macropolitical goal of the mass faculty layoffs that took place as soon as this law was enacted is obvious: to increase the profits produced by the education sector exponentially. This is accomplished by means of two interrelated measures: a reduction of salaries for contingent faculty hired to substitute the laid-off instructors and a consequent reduction in tuition fees, which allows these private universities to expand their "clientele." The micropolitical goal of these layoffs, however, is less obvious.

During the Workers' Party administrations, as the quality of life of the most disenfranchised segments of the population improved, students from historically underrepresented backgrounds began enrolling in private universities. This contributed positively to the expansion and refinement of the micro- and macropolitical actions taken by these students. But the micropolitical objective of the mass faculty layoffs in private universities was not only to reduce the quality of the education

The New Modality of Coup 119

offered in those universities: the objective was even more perverse. Some of those universities used the decrease in tuition costs as the focus of their marketing campaigns, widely disseminated at around the same time that the layoffs were taking place. Incontestably populist, the narrative of the campaigns led the most disenfranchised segments of the population to believe that access to education had in fact been expanded (when in fact the whole operation put education in a more precarious place). The same populist discourse was used by the federal government to legitimize its revisions to the national education curriculum, through an expansive publicity campaign broadcast several times a day over the course of several months on every conceivable media platform. The Globo network was especially important in the dissemination of this campaign. It was staged during peak hours of the network, in the slots reserved for the most popular evening soap operas.

In the area of land rights, which includes environmental law and laws concerning indigenous land, the same year of 2017 saw then President Michel Temer[63] enact a decree that dissolved the Reserva Nacional do Cobre e Associados (Renca). With more than 4.2 million hectares, and located between the states of Pará and Amapá,[64] this reserve was created towards the end of the military dictatorship in 1984 with the intention of preventing the exploitation of miners by foreign companies.[65] It is populated by indigenous communities and is located in what is known as the Guiana Shield, a 1.7 billion-year-old geological formation that includes part of the Brazilian, Venezuelan, and French Guiana Amazon. The Guiana Shield includes the largest expanse of protected areas in the world, with a rate of deforestation of less than 1 percent. It is home to plant and animal species found nowhere else in the world.

The dissolution of the Renca reserve was intended to open the region to domestic and international private investment, especially from mining corporations. And, from a macropolitical point of view, this dissolution was a failure.[66] President Temer was forced to ditch his plans for the reserve after facing immense national and international pressure, and not just from the environmental sector. Temer went on to announce a new decree with similar language, but this new decree was investigated by Brazilian justice officials and it was eventually abandoned. But despite the failure of this measure at the macropolitical level,

120 The New Modality of Coup

what remains clear in this debate is that the micropolitical operation dismissing and disqualifying the indigenous peoples who lived in those regions formed part of the larger macropolitical strategy. More widely speaking, the decree clearly revealed what the micropolitical paradigm of the colonial-capitalistic regime is: the abuse of life, not just of human life, not just of the life of a region, but of the life of the whole planetary ecosystem.

Conservatism is Indispensable for Globalitarian Capitalism

Now we can scrutinize more carefully the micropolitical operation of the new modality of the coup proper to globalitarian financialized capitalism. We can also examine why it is necessary to incite conservatism (as an essential element of power) in order to complete this operation. In the first season of the series, the fragility already present in subjectivities (the fragility caused by the old expropriation of their force of creation) is sharpened by the insecurity stirred by the demonization of both the governing left and the ghost of an economic crisis. In the second season, the sense of insecurity intensifies with the rising demonization of the political and entrepreneurial classes, denounced as they are in the most apocalyptic of tones for their perceived role in the economic crisis and for their perceived blame in the institutional crisis that unravels the state as a whole. All this leads subjectivities to latch onto any promise of stability and safety and, further, it leads subjectivities to project their malaise onto scapegoat figures, the same figures now cast in the role of villains. Up to that point, villains were always played by two kinds of characters: politicians accused of corruption (who can then be used as screens, where subjects can project their malaise vis-à-vis the state) and part of the entrepreneurial class (where subjectivities can project their class hatred). The stigmatization of modes of existence that do not fit with the dominant modes of existence (these misfit modes can no longer be reduced to class categories) allows for the malaise to be projected onto them as well.

To summarize, the malaise is not just projected onto the political and the entrepreneurial classes; it is projected onto any segment of society that does not conform to the dominant mode

The New Modality of Coup   *121*

of being, as if this mode were the highest stage of the human condition. When these divergent segments get demonized, alterity itself also gets demonized, which leads to a further reinforcement of subjectivities already hardened vis-à-vis their vital experience. Because this experience is the result of the effects of the other on our bodies, these effects, now demonized, become enormously powerful imaginary threats, and they must be repressed at any cost to avoid the risk of absorbing them. This has the power to demobilize even further the potency of transfiguration of collective reality. The experience of inhabiting the relational fabric woven between different modes of existence carries this potency whenever the destiny of the drive lies in our hands. And this, in sum, is how conditions are created for desire to surrender itself further and more joyfully to the colonial-capitalistic abuse of the vital drive.

The final episodes of the second season of the series, then, show the simultaneous intensification of a macropolitical operation (the dismantlement of the constitution, of the government's social agenda, and of the national economy) and a micropolitical one (the production of subjectivities that give themselves over to the pimping of desire). With that double and complementary operation, society is prepared for what is likely a third and last season: the total command of political and economic power by globalitarian capitalism, established in Brazil for more than a few decades now but still facing a few "inconvenient" obstacles. When this last season in the series begins, society will finally be ready to welcome with open arms the new fold of the regime that conquered the face of the Earth with its imperial power. The regime will be regarded as a "civilized" savior that will rescue the country from its subjective and institutional crisis, cleanse the economy of its shortcomings, and reestablish the dignity of public life, bringing back the nation's lost prestige and the serenity of its citizens. If this scenario takes shape, the coup will be victorious and the series will come to an end.

The Mask of Democratic Legality

In order to arrive at this programmatic grand finale, any and all obstacles that could interrupt or slow down the circulation of capital, of information, and of people must be eliminated.

122 The New Modality of Coup

Obstacles exist on all of capital's pathways, and the nature of these obstacles is varied: people, groups, ethnicities, institutions, services, workspaces, borders, countries, laws, imaginaries, habits, modes of existence, types of sexuality, artistic practices, and activist movements. All these can constitute, in some way or another, obstacles for the free circulation of capital. Obstacles in the circulation of capital are therefore not limited to figures that can be neatly understood as the mere polar opposites of capital. This makes the notion of the "enemy" as configured in the Western tradition obsolete in this context. Creating a new figure for the "enemy" is one of the strategies of the new modality of power of the colonial-capitalistic regime. Through its perverse manipulation of the media, the regime creates a notion of enemies that is variable and varied. Anyone who constitutes an obstacle gets dressed up as a villain and turned into a target for the masses to satisfy their appetite for destruction. This will last only for a brief period of time, long enough to eliminate these obstacles. Quickly, though, new obstacles will be identified and cast in the role of villains. What we have is a growing cluster of villains at the heart of the script of the series, which changes and varies for the voyeuristic enjoyment of the spectators of this series.

Democracy and the rule of law – which were just beginning to find their grounding in Latin American countries when the series made its debut – are some of the largest macropolitical obstacles standing in the way of financialized globalitarian capitalism. The same micropolitical operation used against the new notion of enemies is deployed against this macropolitical obstacle. But even though the strategy used for these two types of obstacle is the same, the roles are astutely inverted. Instead of being denounced as what they really represent for the authors of the coup – obstacles for the total installation of a capitalist regime – democracy and the rule of law are expeditiously used as war flags in a crusade for the moralization of the nation. Democracy and the rule of law are made to play the role of damsels in distress, and anyone who can be accused of representing a real or fictitious threat to them is cast as an enemy. By the end of the second season of the series as it played out in Brazil, the role of this kind of enemy will be played by a large segment of economic and political leaders. This is when transnational capitalism comes into the scene as the only savior on the planet capable of

The New Modality of Coup 123

rescuing democratic legality, on the condition that it is given full oversight of the whole nation. And this is the character assumed by the regime over the narrative arch of the series, which allows it to hide the fact that, in reality, the regime is the true agent of the coup whose objective is to eliminate the democratic character of the rule of law.

The mask of democratic legality that transnational financialized capitalism wears is subtle, astutely composed. The second season of the series gets released by the media as soon as the first season is over. The scripts are identical; only the characters that play the role of corrupt villains change. In the first season, a segment of Brazilian society could still see that what was really taking place was a coup whose intention was to destroy the image of progressive politicians so as to make possible their removal from power. Once the cast of characters in the series changes in the second season of the series, once a new set of villains has been identified, most people in Brazil begin to believe that the removal from office of progressive politicians was an impartial and dignified action, driven by the need to bring morals back to public life (this is what justifies the reactionary, populist appropriation of the fight against corruption, which turns attention away from the antidemocratic carnage that's really at play). This belief trickles down and contaminates even those who have the least access to rights, the same, vast majority of Brazilian society that benefited from the policies of progressive governments[67] and that once saw the leaders of these governments as their allies. By the end of the second season of the series, once all politicians have been turned into villains, the enemy becomes politics and therefore the state itself.

There is a triple advantage in all of this. The first is to discredit the state in its current structure, so that urgent restructuring becomes the slogan of the moment, embraced by most of the population. This sets the stage for the demand for restructuring to be gloriously addressed by the neoliberal agenda. The second advantage is the de-politicization of society. The defense of civil rights is no longer believed to be guaranteed by citizen participation in democratic institutions, given that these institutions are now perceived to be intrinsically tainted by corruption and invariably populated by thieves, all of them cut from the same rotten cloth. Most concerning here is that de-politicization in the realm of the rule of law completely flattens the social drive

124 The New Modality of Coup

towards an autonomous struggle, micro- or macropolitical, vis-à-vis the state. The third advantage is the heightened fragility of subjectivities, which makes it easier for their potency to be pimped out in a process of abuse interpreted as if it were an act of protection and a guarantee of safety.

Summarizing

The new type of coup, corresponding to globalitarian neoliberal capitalism, consists in a complex set of micro- and macropolitical operations that kill more than two birds with one stone. Anyone and everything that crosses the path of transnational capital is eliminated in the series of operations that constitute the coup. Leftist politicians and the progressive imaginary associated with them are eliminated because they constitute impediments to the dismantlement of the constitution, to privatizations, and to the complete surrender of the nation to transnational financialized capital and its local stakeholders. Conservative politicians explicitly or implicitly aligned with slave-holding values are also eventually eliminated, given their nationalist senility, their ignorance, and their incompetence, and given their despicable need for a blown-up state they can feed from. Part of the local entrepreneurial class is also eliminated, not just because it constitutes a nuisance for transnational financial conglomerates but also because these local entrepreneurs prioritize investments in production and therefore waste opportunities for speculation. Lastly, the state itself in its democratic and/or nationalist version is eliminated. All of this is fueled, micropolitically, by the neutralization of the thinking, creating, collective potency of action that, if it wasn't neutralized, would mobilize in the face of this intolerable scenario.

In short, the new modality of the coup d'état is really nothing other than a coup against the rule of law and democracy itself. It is a coup against society (in its demands in the macropolitical sphere), and, even more radically, it is a coup against life itself (i.e., it is a micropolitical coup), not just human life, individual and collective, but the life of the planet as a whole. Transnational capitalism emerges victorious from all of this, with clean hands. In all likelihood, this is the apotheotic final scene of the coup series we've been outlining here.

The New Modality of Coup   *125*

Trauma and its Destinies

There are two possible, unplanned effects brought about by the series. Both are incipiently manifest towards the end of the second season, after the spell cast by the disguised coup against Lula in the first season of the series is broken and, most importantly, after the establishment of a traumatic level of helplessness in subjectivities following these events. The strategies of desire mobilized in the face of trauma are various. Let's focus on the two extreme poles of the spectrum defined by these strategies in their expansive variation, from the active to the reactive. These are, of course, obviously fictional poles. Desire oscillates between different positions throughout an existence, and elaboration processes have the power to shift initial reactive positions into more active ones, the same way that situations that call forth reactivity have the power to derail responses by desire that were once grounded in an active position.

When desire is grounded on the most reactive pole, we deploy defensive strategies that lead us to protect the status quo, tooth and nail. This is a pathological response, corresponding to someone who has succumbed to trauma, and it depotentializes us. At the other extreme of the spectrum, on the active extreme, our gaze is expanded, and this allows us to be more capable of accessing the subjective effects that violence has on our bodies. It also makes us both more capable of being precise in our deciphering and in our expression and more apt to invent ways to combat violence as it affects our bodies. The creating force is thus mobilized in a way that allows the vital drive to complete its ethical destiny: to transform the status quo, dissolving everything that produces violence against life. This is a healthy response that protects us from giving in to trauma, and it not only preserves our potency but tends to intensify it.

The first response, which results from desire's reactive strategy, tends to lead subjectivities to identify with conservatives, which in turn leads to fervent and euphoric support for conservative figures. As the permanence of conservatives in government stretches out in the second season of the series, and as their support from the masses increases (gassed up by strategists of the coup), conservatives end up being elected to more and more legislative posts, and they manage to establish themselves firmly

126 The New Modality of Coup

and effectively in the halls of power. This is worsened when conservatives are elected to the executive branch of the republic, which has already happened in several different countries. The most significant example of this kind of victory is the election of Donald Trump – a psychopathic buffoon and nationalism peddler – to the presidency of the United States.

It's worth remembering that nationalism is one of the elements of the populist discourse as deployed by the henchmen of financialized capitalism. It is used by the regime as it constructs an image of a "common enemy" that must be eliminated, which justifies and legitimizes the coup (contemporary European anti-immigration policies and the accompanying, virulent spirit of anti-Europeanism both play out in this same key). Conservative, nationalist henchmen are expected to adhere to the agenda of financialized capitalism. Their disobedience is the first collateral effect of the series that was not foreseen in the script. And all of this leads one to believe that this is exactly what will happen if Jair Bolsonaro's bid for the presidency of Brazil is successful, given the level of psychopathy manifest in his figure.[68]

The second response results from desire's active strategy and does not succumb to the trauma. On the contrary, it manages to confront it, generating conditions for the emergence of a new modality of resistance, created collectively vis-à-vis the new modality of power. This is the second collateral effect of the series that also was not foreseen in the series' script. Because it infuses oxygen into the lethal atmosphere that now surrounds us, because it allows us to breathe, let's conclude with some comments regarding this second kind of response.

The New Modality of Resistance

After the first few episodes of the second season of the series (during which the coup will be convincingly portrayed as something other than a coup), the next episodes won't be as popular among audiences. These are the episodes that portray the destruction of democratic advances, the criminalization of cultural creation, the persecution of modes of being linked to minorities, and the disqualification of politics in its entirety. More members of the disenfranchised majority begin to come to terms with the state of misery brought about by the government.

The New Modality of Coup 127

Aside from this, more segments of society begin to realize the dangers that capitalist globalitarian power brings with it, not just for the continuity of human life but for the planetary ecosystem as a whole. An alarm call goes off that makes it more likely for the veil to be removed: the veil disguising the true nature of the abuse. A sense of urgency emerges in subjectivities, and it makes them more likely to fight for access to the subjective experience of our condition as living beings. Subjectivities once again rise up to take the drive back into their own hands. This tends to lead desire to stop cooperating with the submission of the drive-potency for the purposes of abuse. It leads it to act in the direction of transfiguring the present, thus putting a stop to the carnage.

The fact that capitalism in its new fold acts more openly in the micropolitical sphere originates a new modality of resistance: there is growing awareness of the need to also resist in that same micropolitical sphere. This is evident in the new type of social movements that have been destabilizing – here, there, and everywhere – the power of financialized capitalism to determine, on a global level, the modes of existence most expeditious for its interests. The dissemination of this kind of resistance (which has intensified after the tsunami of new coups brought about by the regime all over the planet) has been especially widespread among the younger generation, and even more so in marginalized areas of large urban centers. Especially noteworthy are women's movements (a new fold of feminism), LGBTIQ+ movements (another new fold of struggles, this one in the field of sexualities, where several struggles converge around a number of shared objectives, macro- and micropolitical, refining their strategies, which are no longer reduced to the identitarian demands of the macropolitical sphere), and Afro-descendant movements (in a new fold of struggles against racism). Also noteworthy are indigenous movements and their struggles, which grow wider and wider, more precise, and more interlocked, as well as movements for housing justice. In these last two kinds of movements, strong actions on the micropolitical sphere go hand in hand with their traditional work in the macropolitical sphere. And, in the newly reenvisioned battlefield, the micropolitical field, all of these movements grow stronger.

The irruption of new combat strategies helps us see that the horizon defined by the traditional mode of resistance from

The New Modality of Coup

the left, especially the institutional left, tends to be reduced to the macropolitical sphere, and that this reduction is one of the reasons behind the sense of disorientation and impotence that the left faces in the current state of things. Understanding this provides us with the power not just to jolt ourselves out of the melancholic, fatalistic paralysis that comes over us when we face the somber environment that surrounds us. It also has the power to free us from our resentment towards the left by providing new ways for us to embrace it, by refining our combat instruments in the inextricable spheres of the micro- and macropolitical. These are the instruments offered to us by the new movements.

We know that the larger story behind the narrative arch of financialized capitalism starts well before the three-season series I've outlined here, the series focused on the new modality of coup. We also know that the third season of the last series will be a very long one, that many years will pass before we see the last episode. Perhaps not. Perhaps this last season won't be as long, provided the previous seasons in the series end up materializing expeditiously. Whatever the case is, it's important to note that, whenever financialized capitalism begins to believe in the finality of a last episode for its coup/series, its arrogance starts to blind it. There will never be one last chapter, absolute in its closure, because the only thing that is in fact absolute is life and the struggle between the more active and the more reactive forces: a combat which characterizes life in its essence.

The effects of the coup will be outlined collectively by the clash between the different types of forces at work in this series. To different degrees and in different scales, and with different means of expression, reactive forces promote the abuse of life in its drive-potency of creation. They do so either through the figure of the villain who commits the abuse or through the figure of the victim who cooperates in its own abuse. Active forces, on the other hand (and with the same variation of degrees, scales, and means of expression), promote the affirmation of life's transfiguring potency. They dissolve the existing cast of characters and, in so doing, they also dissolve the scene where these characters act. Active and reactive positions oscillate and combine with each other over the course of individual and collective lives. What's important is the indefatigable labor of struggling against reactive forces within us and in our environment. The success

The New Modality of Coup

of reactive forces will never be guaranteed, and it will never be definitive.

It is impossible to predict the kind of outcomes (which are always provisional) that will emerge from the clash in which we find ourselves at this very moment. These outcomes will be revealed in the third and perhaps last season of the series. But there is a breath of encouragement in the air that comes from the same experience in which we're immersed. It comes from the collective irruption of insubordinate attitudes of the drive vis-à-vis the after-effects of the colonial-capitalistic abuse. Even though this experience is relatively recent, it allows us to imagine other scenarios and to move in the direction of those new scenarios. This is what allows us to believe in the possibility of eliminating the toxic pollution that poisons the atmosphere, at least to a degree sufficient for life to once again flow and thrive.

Eliminating the pollution in our atmosphere is a micropolitical task. It entails a collective labor of decolonizing the unconscious. The focus of the unconscious is the politics of the production of subjectivity that guides both desire and the consequent formations of the unconscious in the social sphere. This is the task we must face in the present moment. Whatever comes later will come later: new forms of existence will establish themselves, with new tensions between different qualities and different intensities of active and reactive forces and their clashes. These clashes, on their part, will call for new insurrection strategies and for the creation of new scenarios, in the endless clash of what we call life.

Postscript

In 2018, soon after I wrote the preceding essay and right before I submitted the book to the Brazilian press in charge of its first, Portuguese-language edition, a new episode of the second season of the series was released. It focused on the sentencing of ex-president Luiz Inácio da Silva (Lula), who was condemned to twelve years and one month in prison for his involvement in Operation Car Wash. Even though this episode was one of two predictable climaxes in the plot of the series, and even though it was likely the last episode of the second season of the series, its

130 The New Modality of Coup

impact on the life of Brazilian society led me to add a postscript to this essay.

Four years later, I started preparing the book for its publication in English. The third season in the series had already taken place; it focused on the construction of Bolsonaro as presidential candidate. A new series we might call "The Coup II" was about to be broadcast. It began in 2021, two years after Bolsonaro's electoral victory. The new episodes confirmed ideas about the new modality of the coup that I had elaborated in the preceding essay, and they also included elements that made it possible for me to make my ideas more precise. One of these ideas, however, proved inadequate: the one suggesting that the elites of financial capitalism were not interested in keeping their henchmen in power after they were finished with the dirty work they were assigned to do: expelling the left from the political stage. Moreover, after rereading the postscript I had originally written for this essay, I realized that, in the heat of the moment, I had placed too much emphasis on some factual details. It's as if I needed to review the facts obsessively, one by one, in search of a thread, a sense of meaning, something that could bring relief to the anxiety brought about by a series of moves related to the coup, each one more perverse. I decided, then, to rewrite this postscript in its entirety, eliminating everything apart from one detail from the original: the analysis of two photographs that went viral on social media and that are related to the episode of the series where Lula goes to prison. Now, with some distance, it seems possible to get more layers of meaning from these photographs, more meaning than I managed to glean initially. This is the starting point and the focus of this new version of the postscript.

In the first photograph, we see Lula being carried on the shoulders of a multitude surrounding him outside the headquarters of the Sindicato dos Metalúrgicos do ABC, the powerful union of metalworkers located in São Bernardo do Campo in Greater São Paulo.[69] The photo was taken as Lula left the headquarters to turn himself over to officers of the Brazilian Federal Police waiting for him outside the headquarters, ready to transport him to prison. In the second photograph, we see Oscar Maroni[70] (a self-proclaimed "nightlife impresario") staging a scene at a large party he was hosting on the occasion of Lula's imprisonment. The party took place in Maroni's Bahamas Hotel

The New Modality of Coup

131

Club, a nightclub known for its appealing "menu" of young sex workers, some of whom are featured on the club's website, where they're seductively presented in poses that embody all the clichés of the "sexy woman." On the night of the party, Maroni opened the doors of his nightclub to anyone who wanted to participate in the macabre celebration, with free beer and free access to his team of sex workers. The photo does not show the multitude gathered for the party, but we can imagine this crowd was markedly different from the one we can see in Lula's photograph.

I decided to highlight these images because they serve as testimony of the macro- and micropolitical facets (the two are indissociably linked) of the events these photographs register. On the one hand, they capture the forms of expression bodies take in each one of the scenes registered by the photographs and the different relationships between the bodies portrayed in those photographs (this is the visible, macropolitical facet of the scenes portrayed). On the other hand, they provide an image of (a body for) the pulse of the forces in play in the events captured by the photograph (this is the invisible, micropolitical facet of the scenes portrayed). The expressive contrast between these photos is micropolitically and macropolitically evident when we see them side by side.

The Visible and the Invisible in the Image of Lula Being Carried on the Shoulders of the Multitude

Read from a macropolitical perspective, the photograph of Lula turning himself over to the police reveals how far the juridical-political farce that imprisoned him managed to go. This stands in contrast to his response to his illegal imprisonment, which was based on his right to defend himself against the accusations. These are two different positions in the macropolitical sphere, and they represent a struggle that cannot be reduced to a simple difference between the right and the left. What's at stake here are two types of relationship to the social pact of democracy. On one of the poles of the spectrum defined by these two types of relationship, what's at issue is a defense of the interests endangered by an encroachment on the law that seeks to legitimize the distortion of facts for the purpose of achieving certain goals. On the opposite pole, what's critical is the framework

132   The New Modality of Coup

© Francisco Proner

© Túlio Vidal

The New Modality of Coup

of constitutional norms that establishes rules for democratic contention. The scene captured in Lula's photo also shows us the response of a segment of Brazilian society that positioned itself against Lula's imprisonment, all of whom were fully aware of the undeniable illegality of the sentence imposed on him.

When we read this photograph from a micropolitical perspective, we feel the pulse of forces that are actualized in the presence of the police officers who carried out Lula's arrest. We don't see these officers, but those with enough knowledge to contextualize the photo know that Lula was heading towards them. What pulsates in this presence are the reactive forces of the macabre plan that led to Lula's prosecution. This was the successful realization of the micropolitical strategy of the new modality of the coup. As I outlined in this essay, this strategy consisted in disguising the illegality of the coup with a mask of legality (a so-called soft coup), legitimized by the abusive manipulation of facts that takes place in the series. The intent of these manipulations was to abduct the mind of spectators, separating words from their souls. As I mentioned in the prelude to this book, the Guarani teach us that the separation between souls and words is the source of all illnesses. The cognitive collapse that results from this separation is the disease of the soul that makes possible the mobilization of reactivity in the social body, which is necessary to secure support for the coup.

In contrast to these forces, we can also sense active forces in the photograph, forces actualized in Lula's attitude, which embodies his potency, and which did not succumb to the trauma of the diabolic image that this plot tried to attach to him: a potency that did not succumb even in the face of the prison term that he was facing. Active forces are also embodied in the image of the multitude that surrounds Lula warmly, on all sides: the forces molded in the arms stretching out towards Lula, as if to hug him, and in the shoulders offered to carry him. The potency of those who did not succumb to the spell of manipulations, of those who did not allow their minds to be abducted and their expression to be stripped of soul, pulsates in these gestures. These gestures actualized the memory of sensations linked to the unquestionable improvement in living conditions provided by the governments of the Workers' Party. In other words, those present in this photo did not succumb to the pathological effects that the manipulations of the coup sought to produce, effects

134 The New Modality of Coup

that, at that time, had already reduced the number of people supporting Lula, from 85 percent (the highest approval rating he enjoyed during his administration) to 25 percent.

The Visible and the Invisible in the Image of the Pimp Celebrating Lula's Imprisonment

If we read the other photo from a macropolitical perspective, Maroni's attitude and the bash he threw to celebrate Lula's imprisonment provide us, on their part, with expressions of the other segment of Brazilian society, the segment that identified with the plot of the coup, the one that celebrated the success of this plot. Read from a micropolitical perspective, the photograph embodies the pathological effects of the manipulations related to the coup and performed on the subjectivity of these segments of society, the same segments that allowed themselves to be abducted. It also embodies the reactive forces that pulsate in these segments' response to the pathological effects of the coup. It's worth noting that a segment of Brazilians who succumbed to this captivity come from social sectors that benefited from the social agenda of the governments of the Workers' Party. These Brazilians not only had their mind abducted by the micropolitical operation of the series; they also had their memories held hostage, leading to a kind of blackout.

In this photograph, we see Maroni dressed as a prisoner, an obvious and demeaning allusion to Lula's imprisonment. He holds in his arms one of the sex workers employed by his "enterprise"; she is naked from the waist down, wearing nothing but boots (that classic fetish object) and a string thong pressed between her thighs (a piece of underwear that was likely torn away from her by Maroni, to expose the woman's body for the enjoyment of the partygoers). One of Maroni's hands covers the face of the woman, forcefully pushing back her head. The manifest, concrete violence of this gesture not only strips the woman of the possibility of moving; it also strips her of the ability to see and to situate herself visually in this scene. A gesture such as this one actualizes the pulse of sovereignty that this man exerts over the woman who co-stars in the scene: he reduces her to the condition of an object, exhibiting her to the avid eyes of the men who joyfully participate in the revelry (revelry that, we must note, did not

The New Modality of Coup

135

include a single woman who was not there in her capacity as sex worker, a fact that cannot be ascertained with this photo alone but that is registered in other photos of the party that circulated on social media). And there is a third character that takes part in this scene: a man, a sound operator, whose presence and voyeuristic gaze (directed at the pair formed by Maroni and the sex worker) serve as a reminder of the presence and gazes of everyone else who was at the party. The whole scene is reminiscent of an animal auction, where beasts for sale are forcibly immobilized, the better to show off the quality of their flesh and seduce potential buyers.

The obscenity of the performance is a perfect portrait of machismo in its most brutish expression. If machismo corresponds to the tradition of patriarchy, dominant in all Western and Westernized societies, this same machismo is viscerally impregnated in the DNA of Brazilians, and it manifests itself unabashedly, as it does elsewhere in every so-called "former colony." This tradition, which is always latent, and which is actualized in different ways throughout history, is based precisely on a pimping of life that goes well beyond the relational dynamics proper to sex commerce (the sphere where the word "pimping" originated). This same tradition, moreover, goes well beyond its expression in machismo. As I insist not just in this essay but in the other essays that make up this book, pimping defines the dynamic of a relationship to life (not just human life) produced under the regime of the colonial-racist-patriarchal-capitalist unconsciousness, a dynamic that is indissociable from the production of a certain mode of subjectivation that takes place in this same regime and in its formations in the social field. The image in the photo embodies the forces that pulsate in that mode of subjectivation I referred to (in the Prelude to this book) as a structural neurosis, the dynamic of which keeps us imprisoned in a bulletproof kind of narcissism, a necessary condition for the establishment of the accumulation of social capital as the main object of desire.

The legitimacy that machismo has achieved in the sinister scenario now extant in Brazil pulsates in the freedom and in the brashness with which machismo is exhibited in the photograph. Evident in the photo is a classist hatred linked to machismo and directed not just towards Lula but also towards the left in general – towards its social agenda, and towards the democratic

136 The New Modality of Coup

state more generally. The legitimacy that this hatred has achieved (not just among Brazilians who always harbored this sentiment, but also among part of the 85 percent of Brazilians who had previously supported the governments of the Workers' Party) also pulsates in the photo.

But the whole thing does not stop there. Visible in the photograph are two portraits hanging on a wall behind Maroni, the sex worker, and the sound operator gazing at the former two. One of these portraits shows a man wearing a suit and tie; the other shows a woman wearing a pearl necklace. The lower part of these portraits traces a horizontal line; this line divides the composition of the photograph. The man and the woman in those portraits (the man in the suit and tie and the woman wearing pearls) occupy the higher portion of the photograph, while the three characters physically present in Maroni's party and included in the photograph occupy the lower portion. This makes it seem as if Maroni, the sex worker, and the sound operator are inferior, standing below the figures in the portraits. Everyone else attending the party and celebrating Lula's conviction (but not pictured in the photograph) also occupy the lower part of the image. The faces of the people portrayed in the display are disproportionate relative to their bodies, and this contributes to the sense of superiority of these figures in relation to the trio physically present and pictured at the party. Both groups of people represented in the photograph (the man and the woman pictured in the gigantic display; the three people present in Maroni's party) are perfectly aligned in the middle of the photograph, along a vertical axis.

The man in the suit and tie is Sergio Moro, the federal judge involved in Operation Car Wash, the same one who sentenced Lula to prison. The woman wearing pearls is Cármen Lúcia Antunes Rocha, who at the time presided over the Supremo Tribunal Federal (the highest court in Brazil) and who postponed the habeas corpus petition made to guarantee Lula's freedom of movement. To justify her decision, she appealed to a single precedent, the case of prisoner who remained in prison even while his case was being appealed in a process that contravened the presumption of innocence that must be maintained until all appeal procedures have been exhausted, as guaranteed by the Brazilian constitution. This postponement turned out to be crucial because it strengthened the supposed legality of Lula's

The New Modality of Coup

imprisonment, eliminating his right to participate in the electoral process, which was the main intention of this whole operation.[71] Judge Cármen Lúcia Antunes Rocha is the only woman shown who is not a sex worker: she is a woman in power, representing a prestigious public institution, who participated actively in Lula's imprisonment, in contrast to the sex worker, subject as she is to the objectification that makes possible her abuse, all as a part of celebration of Lula going to prison.

One last detail is worth considering: the portraits of Moro and Antunes Rocha were commissioned by Maroni as decorations for his bash. The intention, according to him, was to pay homage to the two characters that, in the series we're calling "The Coup," rose to the status of new national heroes, for their contributions to the imprisonment of the alleged "gang of criminals"[72] formed by politicians from the Workers' Party and their leader, Lula. The presence of these portraits in the photograph functions as another element in the fetid performance that took place during the party: it expresses not just the form of the coup produced by the series in the macropolitical sphere but also its micropolitical effect.

What Does the Contrast Between These Two Images Reveal?

When we place these photos side by side, the operations of the new modality of the coup in the macro- and micropolitical spheres become more visible. The operation in the macropolitical sphere that annulled Lula's right to run for office is expressed in the first photo, in the presence of the police officers who showed up to enforce Lula's prison sentence, the same sentence made possible by the judges whose portraits served as decorations in Maroni's party. The blown-up images of these judges floating above the scene of Maroni's party are indicative of the central role that the judicial branch played in the success of the series we're calling "The Coup." This branch, in turn, worked in conjunction with two collaborators in a triple alliance formed by the judiciary, parliament, and large media corporations, all of them co-responsible (although not always visibly so) for the success of the series. All three institutions (the press, the representative branch, the judicial branch) came together in the service of financialized, transnational capitalism, whose interests are shared by each one of these institutions.

In the micropolitical sphere, the comparison of these photos provides an image that embodies the contrast between the forces actualized in the different responses to the micropolitical operation that, as we have seen, consisted in the mobilization and legitimization of the reactivity of Brazilian society. On the one hand, we have the active forces of the multitude of men, women, and children who came together as a single body to surround Lula and to accompany him in his decision to turn himself in and respect the prison sentence imposed upon him. On the other hand, we have the reactive forces of the multitude of machos reeking of beer; they are not visible in the photo with Maroni, but their presence is mirrored in the avid, voyeuristic gaze of the sound operator. They all share in the joy brought about by the victorious imprisonment of Lula.

A (Not So) Strange Coincidence

As I rewrote this postcript, I realized that there is an evident similarity between the photo featuring Lula, taken in April 2016, and another photo taken on September 6 of that same year,

© Infografia/Poder360

The New Modality of Coup   139

during Bolsonaro's presidential campaign. In this image, we can see another multitude, this one surrounding Bolsonaro, the then presidential candidate, and carrying him on their shoulders. The composition and framing of these two photographs is almost identical. The one showing Bolsonaro went viral on social media, because the same day that it was taken Bolsonaro was stabbed in the abdomen by Adélio Bispo de Oliveira. Assuming that the similarities between the images are not a coincidence, I decided to incorporate the one with Bolsonaro to explore these similarities and to add this image to my analysis.

Several conspiracy theories emerged in the aftermath of Bolsonaro's stabbing, both from the left and from the right. Fake news generated by the right proliferated on social media, attributing the incident to an assassination attempt coordinated by parties on the left, most visibly represented by the Workers' Party and by PSOL (the Socialismo e Liberdade party). This, in turn, led to death threats against and the persecution of several people linked to these parties, among them Jean Willys, at the time a federal representative affiliated to PSOL (Willys ended up in exile in Europe, such was the nature of the threats made against him). Even though these conspiracy theories were quickly debunked, they still manage to become imprinted in the minds of Brazilians.

The left, for its part, interpreted the stabbing as a plot to guarantee Bolsonaro's victory, a victory that at that time was not a done deal even though Lula had already been expelled from the political scene. A slow-motion video of the incident that circulated online seemed to corroborate this theory. The video seems to show the security guards protecting Bolsonaro gesturing towards Adélio, the man who stabbed Bolsonaro, in a way that suggested that those same guards were coordinating with the perpetrator, directing him at first to wait, and eventually indicating the right time to act. This was all followed by what appeared to be motions on the part of the security guards that made it easier for Adélio to get close to Bolsonaro. Mysteriously, the video disappeared from the internet soon after it was first made available.

From the perspective of the micropolitical strategy conceived in the coup series, the re-creation of the exact same scene Lula initiated as he turned himself in to go to prison, but with Bolsonaro substituting Lula in an electoral event, carries the

140 The New Modality of Coup

power of capturing the affect mobilized by Lula and rerouting this same affect to associate it with Bolsonaro. The extraction and exploitation of affect associated with Lula did not begin there: it started earlier, in previous and successful operations that managed to transform the image of a leader beloved by more than 80 percent of Brazilians into the image of a supposed criminal, someone who betrayed the trust of those who had placed their hopes in him. The new leader that now occupies the place Lula once had, the leader now being carried on the shoulders of a multitude, is transformed into a kind of messiah sent from heaven to save Brazil – and thus the Brazilian people – from the sins of corruption (coincidentally, Messiah is one of Bolsonaro's given names). The strategy is completed with the use the gang of henchmen led by Bolsonaro gave to the stabbing incident: by alleging that members of the left were behind the assassination attempt, the manipulation of affect was mobilized even more intensely. The voices calling for the myth of Bolsonaro grew more and more numerous.

It's interesting to note that, in the testimony he provided and in letters he wrote from prison, Adélio, the man who stabbed Bolsonaro, refers to the latter as the Antichrist, the name given in the Bible to the false messiah sent by Satan to usurp the place of Christ before he returns to Earth. Now, if we consider the fact that delirium is a mode of enunciating affects mobilized in the body of a schizophrenic through historical circumstances, Adélio's delirium can be said to enunciate the fact that he saw Bolsonaro as a false messiah destined to take the place of Lula (the latter raised, from Adélio's perspective, to the position of Christ), who would be returning to the political stage after the "crucifixion" of his imprisonment. Considered from this point of view, Adélio's gesture can be said to have been driven by the desire to eliminate a false messiah from the scene. Contrary to what Adélio might have intended, his stabbing of Bolsonaro corroborated the idea of Bolsonaro as an embodiment of the true messiah, as Christ himself returning to Earth to save Brazil from the so-called gang of criminals who led Brazil for two decades.

The construction of the narrative that raises Bolsonaro to the status of messiah, that transforms him into a mythical being, reaches deep into the Christian imaginary held dear by most Brazilians, especially those affiliated to evangelical churches, which have played a micropolitical role in capturing the

The New Modality of Coup 141

subjectivity of their members (a role that has grown more intense in recent years during Bolsonaro's administration; evangelicals now constitute 35 percent of the Brazilian population). Beyond the manipulation of affects, the stabbing had the advantage of justifying Bolsonaro's absence from the last set of televised debates, which in turn ended up protecting his mythical image; the debates that had already taken place had exposed the absolute stupidity of his pathetic figure.

Three seasons' worth of maneuvers produced in the series called "The Coup" ended in success: Jair Bolsonaro won the presidential elections held in October 2018.

The Shot Backfired

Lula was freed in 2021, after spending 580 days in prison, following a decision made by the same court (the STF, the highest court in Brazil) that had earlier upheld his imprisonment. More recently, in 2022, this same court annulled all previous criminal sanctions against Lula linked to Operation Car Wash, and it ordered all criminal proceedings to be restarted by a different part of the federal court system. Annulment of the criminal sanctions levied against Lula restored his political rights, allowing him to run for president once again in 2022.

That this decision for annulment was taken at the time it was taken is no coincidence; it could well have been issued three years before, when hacked recordings from the Telegram app became public, recordings that documented conversations between those responsible for Operation Car Wash that made evident the bias of Judge Moro and that revealed the political trap set by Judge Moro and by the prosecutors involved in that same operation. The reason why the annulment decision was made at that time was that, in 2021, three years into Bolsonaro's presidency, the elites of transnational, corporate, financialized capitalism realized that they were losing control over the effects of the series – which is to say that they were losing control over the coup. Their shot backfired.

This was all foreseen by the essay that precedes this postscript, which was written a few months before Bolsonaro's victory. At the time, I pointed out the fact that the henchmen of the series (the figures put in power to expel progressive forces from the political scene) would end up liking the positions

142   The New Modality of Coup

they had recently conquered and would wish to consolidate themselves in those positions. This went against what was originally intended for them, which was to keep them in power only long enough for them to complete their dirty work. I put forward that hypothesis based on what had already taken place in previous episodes of the series, episodes that showed some of these henchmen being prosecuted for corruption and for other crimes that resulted in the stripping of their political rights and their eventual imprisonment.[73]

But the facts that came afterwards led me to revise this hypothesis. Today, I'm inclined to think that the intent behind this project orchestrated by transnational capitalist elites was not (and is not) to expel their henchmen from the political scene; on the contrary, these henchmen are here to stay, and not just in Brazil. To keep them in power is part of the political strategy that has been unfolding in several different countries, a strategy that relies on the right-wing populism cultivated by these characters, a populism that galvanizes reactivity and is able to mobilize resentment against the parties and the leaders of the left. Keeping these henchmen in power, however, is contingent upon an ability to keep them in line, without allowing them to meddle too much in the political and economic agenda that transnational elites want to keep under their control.

In Brazil, the idea was to mobilize resentment against Lula and the Workers' Party among the segment of Brazilian society that had previously supported them. The hope was that this resentment would add to the hatred that a significant portion of the middle and upper classes harbored for Lula and his party from the moment they appeared on the political scene (a class hatred marked by racist contempt). If they achieved this, the makers of the series would be able to take power back from the left, the same power the elites previously held. This is the dynamic that we see unfolding in the rise of the right elsewhere in the world. But something went awry.

The first thing that went amiss was that, once he was in authority, Bolsonaro's psychopathy led him to embrace power as if it belonged to him personally. He became completely derailed from the political and economic agenda that he was elected to oversee – a derailment that was made possible by several members of his government: militiamen of the worst kind and old-guard generals that never got over the end of the dictatorship.

The New Modality of Coup 143

Underpinning all this was the fact that, in Brazil, in contrast to other countries previously under dictatorship in Latin America, members of the military had never faced punishment for their crimes, which kept their legitimacy as public figures intact. Other members of Bolsonaro's government that empowered Bolsonaro's power grab included mediocre representatives of the far right wing.

The second thing that went wrong has to do with the direction that right-wing populism took in Brazil, the same populism that Bolsonaro was expected to steer as a presidential candidate and eventually as president. What was not expected (regardless of how predictable this was, given Bolsonaro's trajectory) was that his psychopathy would lead him to a fascist kind of populism. The falsification of reality promoted by the series was so intensified by this fascist populism that a cognitive collapse took place, on top of the mental chaos already harbored by most of Brazilian society. This cognitive collapse prepared the ground for a fascist outbreak. What was expected even less was that the spread of the fascist outbreak would reach a point that allowed for the formation of an organized mass movement of more than negligible proportions, a movement formed by those most acutely infected with fascism.

It's true that this mass movement is useful in the demonization of leftist leaders. But it is also true that the fascist overtone of this movement, the result of its identification with its leader, Bolsonaro, also mobilized the opposite effect. Part of the segments that previously supported Lula (but succumbed to the falsification of facts promoted by the series) went back to supporting Lula.

A Split in the Triple Alliance

Faced with all this, the priority for a segment of those responsible for the coup was to impede Bolsonaro from being reelected, by any means necessary, and to prevent him and his gang from remaining in power. The triple alliance that conceived and directed the plot of the series split apart. On one side of this split there remained the members of the alliance long infected with fascism, the ones who were fascist long before the current outbreak of fascism. This group includes militiamen

144 The New Modality of Coup

and part of the armed forces that assumed positions of power in the executive, legislative, and judicial branches of Bolsonaro's administration. The group also included members of the Federal Police, part of the middle and upper classes (the most retrograde among business owners in Brazil, particularly agrobusiness owners), the rotten lot of evangelical politicians (by this point they were affiliated to several different parties in Brazil), and the majority in Parliament, conservative and right wing (the so-called *Centrão*).[74]

On the other side of the split we find neoliberals. These include barons of finance and business, members of the judicial branch (specially the STF), and associates of large media corporations. This is the side of the alliance that retained control of the series. Faced with the situation presented by Bolsonaro's government, they decided to end the series quickly and to launch a new series, with the same strategies (strategies for a new modality of the coup) used in the first series but with new characters and a new plot. The new series, which I called "The Coup II," is on air right now.

The plot of this new series is meant to destroy the consolidation of power achieved by the out-of-control bunch of scoundrels: the good guys in the first series who are now presented as the villains of the story. Bolsonaro's gaffes ended up overtaking most of the episodes in the new series, together with the blunders of his allies in government (random secondary characters, small-time bureaucrats who felt empowered to go after the breadcrumbs of this feast of corruption).

The new villains played their newly assigned roles to perfection, given how well their personalities aligned with those roles. This, in turn, made it unnecessary to falsify facts (the way they were falsified in the first series) in order to demonize the new villains and mobilize hatred against them (the hatred necessary to expel them from the political stage). It was enough to document their speech and their acts and to disseminate these documents spectacularly, day in and day out. This renders "The Coup II" more akin to a reality show (Big Brother Brazil comes to mind) than to a narrative series proper.

The new series was successful in its attempt to reduce the mass of Bolsonaro supporters without altogether reducing the hatred previously mobilized against Lula and the Workers' Party. But another twist in the series made it less successful than it might

The New Modality of Coup   *145*

have been. What I have in mind is the intensifying reactivity of Bolsonaro's most ardent supporters. For these subjects, the ones most acutely infected by the fascist outbreak, the movement unleashed by Bolsonaro brought them a kind of legitimacy they had never experienced, both because of their social and their economic background. This was especially the case for Brazilians from the lower middle class, the source of a large segment of those who have embraced the myth of Bolsonaro, which offers them an opportunity to affirm themselves and to somehow see themselves mirrored on the public stage.

Confronted with this scenario, the fascist side of the alliance intensified its strategies related to the falsification of reality, the same strategies aimed at the demonization of the left through a kind of collective lynching ritual that takes place in social media (this side of the alliance is distinctly well versed in the use of social media). The objective here is to win elections by any means necessary. But the neoliberal side of the alliance, who retained control of the series, managed to erect successful barriers against these efforts. But, to do this, it had to overcome an obstacle: as support for Lula grew greater and greater (as a response to the fascist plague), it became evident that Lula was the only viable candidate with a chance of defeating Bolsonaro.

Given this situation, the authors responsible for the script of "The Coup II" attempted to come up with a candidate that could defeat Lula as well as Bolsonaro, but their plans for a so-called third way never got off the ground. They thus had to support (against their wishes and on a temporary basis) Lula as their only way out, as the only viable defense of their interests. This is exactly why the Workers' Party chose Geraldo Alckmin[75] as Lula's running mate, even though Alckmin is a former member of the PSDB, a party that stood in fierce opposition to the Workers' Party during its three administrations.

Lula's administration never actually went against the interest of Brazilian elites; on the contrary, it provided conditions that favored the growth of their fortunes. The subjectivity of these elites, however, is marked by an entrenched, classist form of racism, as well as a sense of domestic xenophobia vis-à-vis certain regions in Brazil. This prevents elites from providing any kind of genuine support for Lula, whose figure and body is inscribed with both racial and regional markers: Lula is

146   The New Modality of Coup

working class, and he was born in Northeast Brazil (*nordestinos* are among the most frequent victims of Brazilian domestic xenophobia).

An Uncertain Future

In October 2022, Lula won the presidential elections by a small margin: he defeated Bolsonaro. After these results, a great sense of relief was experienced by half of the Brazilian population, but it is difficult to foresee what will unfold from the current scenario. It all hinges on some very complex work that must be completed in both the macro- and the micropolitical sphere.

In the macropolitical sphere, it will not be easy to reconstruct state institutions that were demolished during Bolsonaro's administration, especially those linked to the social sector (which includes education, health, labor, housing, food security, etc.), to the cultural sector, to the preservation of the environment, and to the protection of indigenous peoples. These institutions will have to be reconstructed with new architecture in a way that both incorporates the micropolitical sphere and can match the sophisticated manipulation of subjectivity undertaken by the new modality of power. To design this response (this new architecture), the struggles and achievements of contemporary social movements in the micropolitical sphere (movements linked to LGBTQAI+ and environmental activism) will have to be considered. The new architecture will also need to count on an online presence that can match the mastery that the global right has over social media, where the right deploys its principal strategies of micropolitical power.

The challenge we have ahead of us is greater still if we consider the unwelcoming environment where that kind of reconstruction will take place, an environment defined by a global economic crisis, by depleted national coffers after Bolsonaro's administration, and by majorities in state and federal legislatures beholden to the interests of macropolitically and micropolitically reactive forces (though Bolsonaro lost the election, legislators supporting him still managed to get elected and now constitute majorities in legislative bodies throughout the nation). Lastly, and most crucially, the interests of transnational financialized capitalism and their local representatives are still part of the picture; in fact, they've already begun to put

The New Modality of Coup   *147*

pressure on the economic agenda of the new government, and they've been doing so since day one, the day after the election.

In the micropolitical sphere, it won't be easy to dissolve the excessive reactivity mobilized and produced by the two series we've discussed here ("The Coup" and "The Coup II") in the subjectivities of a significant number of Brazilians, the same reactivity behind the collective cognitive collapse we now face. Making matters worse is the mistake made during the first series when Bolsonaro was chosen as lead henchman, a choice that did not anticipate his ability to unleash a fascist outbreak on a social body already weakened by cognitive collapse and vulnerable to conditions that lead to the illness of fascism. Almost half of the population voted for Bolsonaro, and this alone indicates that the new fascist outbreak is far from over. The illness of fascism had never spread like this in Brazil;[76] creating antibodies strong enough to overcome this variant will not be easy.

Sad scenes unfolded after the results of the election were announced. Devotees of the myth of Bolsonaro, unhappy with the loss of their candidate, mobilized throughout the country, denouncing the elections as fraudulent and calling for the return of the military dictatorship. Their methods alternated between roadblocks, encampments outside of military bases, and public prayer sessions featuring people kneeling on the pavement, raising a collective plea to God for a Brazil free from communism. The number of participants in these gatherings varied, sometimes reaching thousands. Attendants tend to wear green and yellow, the national colors, and sometimes they wear the flag itself around their bodies or as a cape that drapes down their back. The most preposterous messages circulate on social media, things as far-fetched as "Aliens claim that they will capture Lula to make way for Bolsonaro's return," or theories regarding the reincarnation of Bolsonaro in Lula's body, or that Lula is dead, that "Lula" is actually an actor wearing a mask of Lula's face.

Bolsonaro remained silent in the days and weeks after the election; he has not, therefore, explicitly supported the behavior of his supporters. The effects of his silence, however, are far from neutral. Bolsonaro's silence raises his supporters to the role of spokespersons for the words and acts of the messiah, which further increases the social and narcissistic capital of these

148 The New Modality of Coup

supporters and which further strengthens their blindness in the face of reality, intensifying their collective hallucinations and stimulating their fervor and their fury. In sum, we are far from a cure for the mass of Brazilians who are gravely ill.

Beyond the challenges we face in the micro- and macropolitical sphere, we cannot forget that the strategy of the soft coup – the one corresponding to the new modality of power – continues in full force.

Let's Get to Work

As I wrote towards the end of this essay, what keeps us breathing amid this dystopian scenario, what keeps us from giving in to desperation and melancholia, is the fact that unconsciousnesses that protest have been spreading and multiplying while this scenario consolidates. This is what I've been affirming, insistently, since the beginning of this book, what I have been saying almost obsessively in this essay and in the other essays that make up this volume. In this protest, lines of flight are drawn, away from the regime of the unconscious that dominates the social and subjective fields.

There seems to be something irresistible here, a genetic mutation, a change in the patriarchal, slavocrat DNA. Even if the belief in this kind of irreversible change is nothing but a chimera, even if it's just a defense mechanism against the trauma caused by the terror of the situation we've been living through over the past few years (the terror remains in the air, despite Lula's victory), the sinister state of our current affairs will still, some day, come to an end. No chapter in the history of humanity is definitive, just as no form of existence – out of the countless forms of existence assumed by every living species – is itself definitive. Life goes on: it persists; it does so in its affirmation of the potency of differentiation, and it does so every time it needs to.

To be conscious of this potency and to participate in the collective work necessary to keep this potency active requires knowing that each new world that emerges entails new challenges, and that these challenges call upon us to participate in the inevitable micropolitical clash that takes place between the different degrees of potency where life manifests itself, from the more active to the more reactive. Forms of reality emerge from this

The New Modality of Coup 149

clash. Knowing this inoculates us from any kind of defensive, messianic rapture. Exorcising these kinds of raptures is part of what the protests of the unconsciousnesses do, and this, in turn, is part of our micropolitical resistance to the power that the racial-colonial-patriarchal-capitalist regime of the unconscious has over the production of ourselves. This power has the capacity to lift us up and away from the vibrational ground constituted by our condition as living beings, and this, in turn, leads us to conceive idealized images of the future which prevent us from facing what is happening to us, impeding us from creating adequate responses to it.

Our fundamental ethical task, as I suggest towards the end of the essay preceding this postscript, consists in facing the challenge of the clash against reactive forces, the same forces that impose themselves on us and outside of us. Affects, evaluating devices for the sensations caused in our bodies by the effects of the forces that constitute an ecosystem (not just an environmental ecosystem but a social and mental one as well), are the greatest compass we can count on to guide desire in this clash. Affects can guide desire from an active micropolitical perspective, so that our actions can rise to the challenge imposed by the demands life makes in the face of these environmental effects.

We must dedicate ourselves more and more to reconnecting with what affects point out to us. Our distance from this kind of knowledge is the principal component of the factory of worlds that operates under the dominant regime of the unconscious. If we don't undo this component within us and outside us, the current scenario will reconstitute itself infinitely, changing nothing but its technologies of manipulation, which work hard to capture desire in such a way that keeps life under the yoke of pimping. Nothing else remains to be said, nothing but this: let's get to work.

Finale

Ten Suggestions for the Practice of Decolonizing the Unconscious

1 **Undo our numbness and become vulnerable to the forces that compose the living body of the biosphere.** The forces I have in mind here are the forces of the various and varying elements that make up the ecosystem, not only the environmental ecosystem but also the social and mental ecosystems. These are the elements with which we constantly interact in our condition as living beings (whether we know it or not). This vulnerability is the strength of our outside-the-subject experience, which consists in feeling the effects that forces have on our bodies, the vital signals emitted by everything that happens to us.

2 **Unblock, increasingly and with greater commitment, our access to the tense experience of the strange-familiar.** This is a tension that arises from the friction between our distinct and simultaneous experience as both subjects (our actual shape) and outside-the-subject (the experience of the embryonic futures nesting in our body, generated by the body's interactions with the forces of the biosphere).

3 **Do not deny the fragility** that results from the instability that the experience of the strange-familiar causes in us. The deterritorialization carried by that experience inevitably destabilizes us.

4 **Do not interpret the fragility of that unstable state and the discomfort it causes** as if they were "bad things." Do not

Finale 151

project phantasmatic readings on this fragility, readings based on the ego's feeling of helplessness in the face of fragility, a feeling that arises when it interprets fragility as a threat of failure and when it interprets as real the imaginary consequences of this threat (repudiation, rejection, social exclusion, humiliation, and, at its worst, madness). These projections carry inadequate ideas about the real cause of this unstable state and the fragility that comes with it: ideas that interpret its cause as a supposed mistake (our mistake or the mistake of others). This always comes hand in hand with toxic feelings of guilt or resentment.

5 **Activate and expand eco-ethological-knowing (intuition) through the whole of our existence:** the kind of knowing that produces adequate ideas about the real cause (losing the sense of the forms where life is embodied in the present vis-à-vis the germinating futures that pulsate in our body) of our unstable state and fragility.

6 **Do not yield to the will to conserve forms of existence,** and do not yield to the pressure these forms exert against the potency of life in its drive towards the production of difference, a drive set in motion every time life is suffocated by the forms of the present. On the contrary, seek sustenance in the thin thread of that unstable state, until the creating imagination can build a body-expression for the virtual futures that demands to be embodied. This allows for the death of agonizing worlds.

7 **Do not interrupt the time corresponding to the creating imagination.** Avoid the risk of intruding on the germination of a world. This interruption makes the imagination vulnerable to expropriation by the pimp-colonial-capitalistic regime, which instrumentalizes life and leads it away from its ethical destiny (i.e., bringing embryonic futures into existence). It is through this deviation that the imagination is captured, subjecting itself to the imaginary that this regime seductively imposes on us. Instead of creating the new (what gives body to embryonic futures), the imagination is reduced to the mere exercise of its creative capacity (dissociated from life and its demands) to produce novelties instead of creating the new. The purpose of this is to multiply the opportunities for the investment of capital and to stimulate the anxiety to consume, thus increasing the accumulation of capital

152   Finale

(not just economic capital but also social and narcissistic capital).

8 **Do not renounce desire in its active potency (in its life-affirming ethics).** This entails keeping life as fecund as possible, as well as keeping up with the vital potency of differentiation (of forms of existence and of their respective values).

9 **Do not negotiate the non-negotiable.** Do not negotiate with anything that could obstruct life's affirmation in its active exercising as creating potency. What can be negotiated is, in turn, everything that is acceptable insofar as it does not weaken this potency. In this case, negotiating is what generates objective conditions for an event to emerge: a sign that life is fulfilling its ethical destiny. Learn to distinguish between the non-negotiable and the negotiable.

10 **Practice thought in its full functions**, which are inextricably ethical, aesthetic, political, critical, and clinical. When we practice thought in this way, we can reimagine the world in each gesture, each word, in each mode of existing and of relating with the other (the human and nonhuman other). Practice thought in this way whenever life requires you to do so.

Notes

1 This epigraph is composed of three fragments from a book by Gilles Deleuze and Félix Guattari, *What is Philosophy?* (New York: Columbia University Press, 1994): 32–3; 34; 23.
2 *Mensalão* is the term given to a bribery scheme that consisted in monthly payments to representatives linked to the political alliance that constituted the government of Luiz Inácio da Silva (Lula). Without these monthly bribes, the projects proposed by the executive branch, especially those linked to its social agenda, would have almost certainly been vetoed by Congress. Although, of course, this kind of scheme must be denounced, it's worth noting that this is a political practice endemic to Brazil, and that no one had been processed (much less punished) for it in the history of the republic. The scheme was made public in 2004, and after that a number of prison sentences were issued by Judge Sergio Moro against Workers' Party politicians and their allies, as well as business people involved in the scheme. Lula was condemned to prison in 2017; he was arrested in 2018 and remained in prison for 580 days. In 2022, decisions made as part of the legal process of Operation Car Wash were nullified. The invalidation was based on three arguments. The third one pointed to the flagrant partiality Judge Moro exhibited during his handling of the Lula case. Lula's political rights were restored, and this, in turn, allowed him once again to run for office. For more on this saga, see the last essay in this book.
3 The term "globalitarian" was proposed by the Brazilian geographer Milton Santos (1926–2001), the author of more than forty books

154 Notes to pp. xxi–xxv

published in Brazil and elsewhere. The notion of "globalitarianism," which fuses together "globalization" and "totalitarianism," consists, according to Santos, in a process of universal colonization operated by capitalism in its current phase, which deepens the rift between the rich and the poor, metropolises and colonies. I would add that this process involves politics of subjectivation operating in all segments of social life; these constitute the micropolitical basis for the production and reproduction of the rift not only in classes and colonial relations but also in relations between supposedly different genders, races, etc.

4 I introduced the notion of pimping as applied to the relation between capital and life (which operates in the micropolitical sphere) in a 2002 essay titled "A vida na Berlinda," in *Trópico: Idéias de Norte e Sul*, an online publication. Since then, I've elaborated on this notion in many of my writings.

5 The prelude to the first edition of this book mentioned the powerful high school student movement that occupied public schools in Brazil (mainly technical schools) towards the end of 2015. Many of the students who participated belong to marginalized segments of the population.

6 I am very grateful to all of those who have worked on translations of these texts into the languages in which they have been published. I am especially grateful to Sergio Delgado Moya, responsible for this translation. His exquisite work, which you now have in your hands, offered me the chance to critically reengage with these essays. I am also very grateful for the many interlocutors who, over the course of the years, have read the different and previously published versions. The list of these interlocutors is long – too long, perhaps, to be included in a footnote. I'll mention only Josy Panão, who has dedicated herself to reading and revising my writings for more than a decade.

7 I am grateful to Ticio Escobar, a Paraguayan thinker active in a transdisciplinary field that includes anthropology, art, philosophy, politics, and human rights. He relayed to me several terms from the Guarani language, in all their rich complexity. These terms carry a certain perspective on the relationship to life, very different from the sad, anthropo-phallo-ego-logocentric perspective that governs our thought, as white Westerners, and that also governs, inextricably, our modes of existence. When we allow ourselves to be affected by these Guarani terms, they provide us with valuable tools to dislodge ourselves from the colonial-capitalistic regime of the unconscious; they provide us, in other words, with valuable tools for the micropolitical struggle against this regime. It is worth noting that Paraguay is the only country in the Americas where an indigenous

Notes to pp. 1–2

language (Guarani) has status as official, national language on a par with the language of the colonizer (Spanish). Guarani is used in everyday contexts by 80 percent of Paraguayan society, including the white middle- and upper-class population.

8 Gilles Deleuze and Félix Guattari, "On *Anti-Oedipus*," conversation with Catherine Backès-Clément, *L'Arc* no. 49 (1972); in Gilles Deleuze, *Negotiations, 1972–1990*, trans. Martin Joughin (New York: Columbia University Press, 1995): 22.

9 The movements that hatched throughout the world over the course of the 1980s and into the 2000s can be classified under three different types. The first is characterized by the specifically micropolitical nature of its actions. One example is the punk movement (which emerged in the mid-1970s in the United States and later in Brazil, at the end of the 1970s and over the course of the 1980s), which distanced itself from the pacifist and romantic optimism of the hippie movement. In Brazil, during that same period, movements of a different, second type gained strength; they are characterized by acting simultaneously and indissociably both in the micro- and in the macropolitical sphere. Among them, the black movement (which has existed since the beginning of slavery) and the feminist movement (which had already emerged by the end of the nineteenth century, persisting since then with highs and lows) both gained a new impetus in the 1980s. Another example is the LGBTQIA+ movement that, in Brazil, began organizing at the end of the 1970s and expanded further and further from the 1980s onwards. In the same spirit, the early 1990s in Brazil saw the emergence of demonstrations that became known as the *Caras Pintadas* protests (1992), attended mostly by young people who, united in their efforts to impeach then President Fernando Collor de Mello, also acted in the micropolitical sphere, a feature that would reemerge even more decisively in the mass protests that took place in Brazil in 2013 and in the high school student movements that took over the streets and more than 200 schools in 2015. An international example of this latter type of movement are the May Day demonstrations that burgeoned throughout the world in 2001. The third type of movement is characterized by acting on the macropolitical sphere. In Brazil, two such movements date back to the early 1980s: *Diretas Já* (1983–4) and the rise of the Workers' Party, the *Partido dos Trabalhadores* (PT) (at the time of its founding, the new party was a catalyzer of both micro- and macropolitical movements, but shortly thereafter it morphed into a more traditional party, reducing its goals to the macropolitical sphere). Closer to the end of the 1980s, social movements – such as the Landless Rural Workers' Movement (*Movimento dos*

156 Notes to pp. 2–4

Trabalhadores Rurais Sem Terra, MTST), as well as its offshoot, the Homeless Workers Movement (*Movimento dos Trabalhadores Sem Teto*, MTST) – begin to emerge, strengthened and organized through the proceedings of the Brazilian Constituent Assembly (1987–8). Other movements (such as the indigenous movement) that had already been in existence for a very long time also gained strength through these same proceedings. A significant effect of all these movements – which can also be seen, in different ways, elsewhere in South America – are the electoral wins of leftist candidates to the presidential office of several of these countries in the early 2000s, after a period of democratic reconstitution following the end of dictatorial regimes in each of those contexts.

10 Among the movements that were conceived in the early 2010s and that ally the micro- and the macropolitical in their actions, we may cite the Arab Spring (2010), Occupy (2011), Movimiento 15-M e Indignados (2011), and, in Brazil, the above mentioned 2013 and 2015 movements.

11 On the matter of this radical transformation of the very notion of work, see the writings of Toni Negri and Michael Hardt, especially the trilogy composed of *Empire* (2000), *Multitude* (2004), and *Commonwealth* (2009). The specific ideas by these authors with which I engage here unfold from the works co-authored by Gilles Deleuze and Félix Guattari: *Anti-Oedipus* (1972) and *A Thousand Plateaus* (1980).

12 See note 11.

13 The notion of "the common" has been broached by various authors from different perspectives. The problematization of this notion in the present volume is presented in dialogue with the perspective adopted by Hardt and Negri. I add an aesthetic and, principally, a clinical dimension to their way of conceiving the construction of the common; both are intrinsic, in my view, to its construction.

14 The idea of an "ethical destiny of the drive," inspired by Jacques Lacan, in the sense suggested here, comes from the work of the Brazilian psychoanalyst and theoretician João Perci Schiavon, who has been in the process of redesigning the architecture of psychoanalysis on the basis of his reading not just of the work of Lacan and Freud but also of the writings by Félix Guattari, of those he co-authored with Gilles Deleuze, and of the philosophical lineage unfolded by these authors. In particular, see his doctoral dissertation, "Pragmatismo Pulsional" (Pragmatism of the drive), defended in 2007 in the PhD program of clinical psychology at the Pontifícia Universidade Católica de São Paulo. The dissertation was revised and published in book form: *Pragmatismo Pulsional* (São Paulo, n-1 Edições, 2019). See also his article, "Pragmatismo

Notes to pp. 20–44

Cultural," *Cadernos de Subjetividade: Revista do Núcleo de Estudos e Pesquisas da Subjetividade* (2010): 124–31.

15 The usual meanings of the term "intuition" tend to be marked exclusively by the perspective of the subject, the perspective to which subjectivity is reduced in our culture, which results in, among other things, logocentrism. From this perspective, any and all modes of deciphering the world that are different from the rationalizing cognitive mode, proper to the subject, are considered inferior. Intuition is even demonized in moments during which its expression excessively threatens the status quo.

16 My approach to the notion of the "drive-unconscious" is drawn from the way in which it has been elaborated by João Perci Schiavon. See note 14.

17 Translator's note: "transduction" is a concept from physics that references the process by means of which energy is transformed into energy of a different nature. The term is also used in genetics and in molecular biology to refer to the process through which genetic material is transferred between cells by means of a virus and with no need for contact between the cells.

18 There is one example of pathologizing the experience of destabilization that comes from psychiatry and is often cartoonish, not to say pathetic: it is the "bipolar" diagnosis used by certain psychiatrists to classify what they consider to be the "disease of artists." From this perspective, the state of suspension where the subjectivity of artists finds itself when it is in the middle of the process of creation (the suspension unleashed by the seed of a world that lives in them but that is yet to find the adequate expression that can bring it into existence) is interpreted as a "depressive" state; the state of vital joy, the ecstasy that comes when this seed finds its form of expression, is interpreted as "euphoric" or "manic."

19 The evangelical movement, of course, exceeds fundamentalism. That is why it is important to specify that what I'm referring to here are the *fundamentalist* type of evangelical churches. There are other strands of the evangelical movement that have undertaken the kind of community work completed extensively and intensely under 1960s and 1970s liberation theology by members of the Catholic Church.

20 Translator's note: the same could be said of the United States, where an "archaic, colonial, and slavocrat mentality" has never ceased to exist, deliberately and strategically redeployed with increased intensity at key moments. It flared up with increased intensity following Donald Trump's most recent entry into presidential politics, which began with his overtly racist questioning of President Barack Obama's nationality in 2011.

158   Notes to pp. 47–52

21 The mediatic-judicial-parliamentary strategy that prepared the ground for the "coup" in Paraguay started in 2008 and was completed in 2012.

22 This fictional narrative manages to cast a spell on mass publics because it resonates with their subjectivity, and not just because this subjectivity is weakened by the threat of a crisis disseminated by this fiction. The basis for the success of the spell rests just as much on the fact that its vital drive is being pimped out and that its structure is decisively marked by the colonial and slave-holding tradition, which nurtures a solid class prejudice, embraced even by those at the bottom of the social pyramid.

23 During the race to elect his successor, towards the end of his term as president of Peru in 2016, Ollanta Humala underwent a character assassination conducted by the triple alliance of the media and the judicial and parliamentary powers, which managed to lower his approval rate substantially, from 57.3 percent towards the beginning of his term to 16 percent by 2016. The race boiled down to the representatives of the two powers that currently dominate the world stage: the investment banker and neoliberal economist Pedro Pablo Kuczynski and the far-right candidate Keiko Fujimori – daughter of ex-president Alberto Fujimori, a distinctly sinister dictator who held power between 1990 and 2000, now serving a 25-year prison sentence after being convicted of corruption, kidnapping, and murder. A campaign as ferocious as the one organized against Humala was mounted against the candidate representing the rise of conservative forces, which handed her rival victory in the election, though the result was almost a draw. Today, Kuczynski is no longer president of Peru: the strategy behind the new modality of the coup d'etat absorbed him. He was removed from office at the beginning of 2018 and was substituted by vice-president Martín Vizcarra Cornejo, who has the backing of Congress and even of Fuerza Popular, Keiko Fujimori's political party. The principal accusation that led to Kuczynski's impeachment was his links to Odebrecht, the Brazilian conglomerate that, not coincidentally, at the time of Kuczynski's impeachment, was performing the part of the scapegoat in the second season of what plays out like a television series produced in real-life Brazil.

24 The term "pollination" was suggested to me by the artist Rolf Abderhalden, founder of "Mapa Teatro" (with Heide Abderhalden) and founder of the interdisciplinary Master's program in Theater and the Living Arts at the Universidad Nacional de Colombia. He notes that the term "contagion" has its origins in the field of medicine, and it is from this field that the term was extracted by sociology. In light of the meanings entailed by the term "contagion"

Notes to pp. 59–62

in relation to the concept of diseases, I will use this term as well as the term "contamination" to describe phenomena related to the proliferation of reactive politics of desire, and I will reserve the notion of "pollination" for phenomena related to the proliferation of active politics of desire.

25 Comité Invisible, *To Our Friends* (South Pasadena, CA: Semiotext(e), 2015): 16.

26 Félix Guattari, *The Three Ecologies*, trans. Ian Pindar and Paul Sutton (London: Athlone Press, [1989] 2000): 27.

27 These are only the most recent examples in a list that dates back much deeper in the past.

28 Translator's note: this essay was originally published in 2018. Since then, left-leaning governments have been elected in Chile and Colombia, expanding a progressive block that includes the government of Mexico and that features the youngest president in the history of Chile and the first Afro-Latina vice-president in the history of Colombia. In Chile and in Colombia, the rise to power of these progressive, left-leaning governments was preceded by long and unprecedented social mobilizations.

29 Although these movements in Brazil began earlier, the more recent historical moment I am flagging here is a period of marked advancement for such movements, in both a quantitative and a qualitative sense. In short, these movements begin to act in the micropolitical sphere, in Brazil and elsewhere. But the fact that their agendas are no longer limited to macropolitical resistance, defined as it is by identitarian struggles, does not mean that they have not continued to mobilize in that sphere, where they've attained significant achievements such as the enactment of laws that protect the rights of women and members of the LGBTQI, black, and indigenous communities, as well as their increased presence in the political scene. One example of this is the candidacy of Sonia Guajajara, an indigenous woman, to the vice-presidency of Brazil in 2018. It's worth noting that these achievements in the macropolitical sphere are far from a sufficient consolidation of the rights of oppressed communities.

30 "Capitalistic" is a term coined by Félix Guattari. The French psychoanalyst works through Karl Marx's idea that capital overcodes trade value, thus subjecting the whole productive process to its ambitions. Guattari extends this idea to encompass the modes of subjectivation that are equally overcodified under the capitalist regime. This results in the silencing of the singular idioms proper to every life. The effects of such silencing is the interruption of becomings – the processes of singularization unleashed in the encounters between bodies and their respective idioms – and the obstruction of the

160 Notes to pp. 63–64

transmutation of reality and the transvalorization of values that these processes tend to produce. With this operation, subjectivities, like the economy, tend to submit themselves to the objectives of the regime, investing these objectives with its own desire, reproducing the status quo in its choices and its actions. The suffix "-istic" the author added to the term "capitalist" refers to that overcodification, one of the medial micropolitical operations of that regime, which bears upon all the domains of human existence. This idea constitutes one of the most innovative and fecund contributions by Guattari. He elaborated it further in his later collaboration with Gilles Deleuze, and since the publication of their *Anti-Oedipus* it stands as one of the principal axes of their co-authored work.

31 It is worth remembering that, by the time Freud was elaborating his theories, studies in ethology were already demonstrating that all species (from the most rudimentary to the most complex) carry with them the capacity for expressive activity, which exceeds the instrumental and adaptive capacities and potentializes them. Since then, several studies have shown that if there is, in fact, anything specific about the expressive capacity in the human species, this specificity has to do with the complexity of human expression and not with any kind of monopoly over this capacity. See, among others, Brian Massumi, *What Animals Teach Us about Politics* (Durham, NC: Duke University Press, 2014).

32 The concept of the "death drive," introduced by Freud, has been the object of a vast range of debates that cut across the whole history of psychoanalysis. It's worth remembering that several approaches to the concept of the drive are already present in the work of Freud himself.

33 Translator's note: Nietzsche's *der Wille zur Macht* has been generally translated into English as a "will to power," but, as Suely Rolnik and others have suggested, the concept of a *will to potency* may, perhaps, more accurately capture what Nietzsche had in mind when he coined this term in German. Note here, for our purposes, the macropolitical dimension of "power," as against the micropolitical aspect of "potency," in as much as the latter (but not the former) can be said to be an essential characteristic of life.

34 Freud managed to decipher the metapsychological dynamic, but he didn't realize, at least not explicitly, that the politics of that dynamic cannot be dissociated from a historical context and, furthermore, that these politics are what gives the metapsychological dynamic its existential consistency, which corresponds to concrete modes of life and their respective symptoms. This vision has since been expanded and refined from different perspectives throughout the history of psychoanalysis and philosophy. The work of Guattari and Deleuze

situates itself in this scope: these authors help us realize that a change in a form of reality and in its respective symptoms is not possible if there are no changes operating on the dominant mode of subjectivation. If we read the work of Freud retrospectively from this perspective, we see that, beyond the unquestionable fact that Freud introduced a deviation from medicine and from the nascent scientific discipline of psychology, there is also in his work a line of flight that is never made explicit but that may well, nonetheless, constitute the most radical turning point of his thought. It consists in a kind of underground potency that carries with it a deviation from Western philosophy (in the modern, colonial-capitalistic tradition) and, more widely speaking, from Western culture – especially from the dominant politics of desire in this culture. From the perspective of that line of flight, Freud favored a reconnection with the knowledge proper to our condition as living beings. Access to this knowledge and to the existential practice guided by this knowledge had been interrupted in the mode of subjectivation that predominates in the modern Western tradition. Moreover, he did this not only at the theoretical level but also and inseparably at the pragmatic level; he did so by introducing a ritual – the clinical psychoanalytic session. The reconnection mentioned above takes place through a long process of regularly scheduled analysis sessions that can be described as "initiatic." This process involves both the simultaneous and inextricable transformation of the dominant politics of subjectivation and the elaboration of psychoanalytic concepts. That said, and contrary to all this, the prevailing tendency in the history of psychoanalysis, as Deleuze and Guattari point out, contributes to the expropriation of the productivity of the unconscious. This productivity is subjected to the theater of Oedipal phantasms, proper to the politics of subjectivation dominant in the colonial-capitalistic regime, which Freud erroneously posited as the universal destiny of the human condition. It is up to us to decolonize psychoanalysis by activating its underground potency, by expanding the line of flight already latent in it from its very beginnings, and by doing this not just in the restricted space of psychotherapeutic practices, and the even more restricted space of the consulting room, but also and most importantly in the whole social field. This implies taking up psychoanalytic practice as an essential instrument of micropolitical insurrection.

35 I proposed the notion of the "colonial-capitalistic unconscious" a decade ago to designate the regime of the unconscious proper to the system that's been in power in the West and in other regions under its colonization for five centuries (the system now in power on the planet as a whole). Recently I realized that my use of this term has

162   Notes to pp. 72–78

precedents in the writings of two authors. The first is Frantz Fanon, who was writing about a "colonial unconscious" as early as the 1950s. I must confess, not without embarrassment, that I began reading the indispensable writings of this author only recently, despite the fact that he's been present in my imaginary since the 1970s, as one of the central figures of the psychiatric and psycho-analytic revolution that took place in those years. The other one is Guattari, who began writing about a "capitalistic unconsciousness" in the early 1980s. The term appears in *Molecular Revolution in Brazil* ([1986] 2007), a book that he and I wrote together; this term, then, was known to me, as would be expected given the fact that I spent four years writing this book (from 1982 to 1986, the year it was first published). Regarding this matter, I must also confess that I only recently recalled the fact that this term already appears in Guattari's *Molecular Revolution*, a fact that probably escaped my memory given how embryonic the effects of this term on my body still were.

36 Félix Guattari, "Integrated World Capitalism and molecular revolution" (1980), presentation at Conference on Information and/ as New Spaces of Liberty (CINEL). Trans A. T. Kingsmith, 2016, at https://adamkingsmith.files.wordpress.com/2016/10/integrated-world-capitalism-and-molecular-revolution.pdf.

37 See note 3.

38 Eduardo Viveiros de Castro flags this tendency in leftist politics in a conversation with Marcio Ferreira da Silva cited by Rafael Cariello in his article "O antropólogo contra o Estado" (*Revista Piauí* no. 88, January 2014). He notes that the Workers' Party (Partido dos Trabalhadores, PT) in Brazil and the left in general are inherently incapable of conceiving any kind of subject beyond the figure of the good worker-turned-good consumer. This translates into an enormous incapacity to understand the populations that refuse to live under the terms of capitalism.

39 The notion of a "protest of the unconsciousnesses" is suggested by Deleuze and Guattari; see Deleuze, *Negotiations, 1972–1990*, trans. Martin Joughin (New York: Columbia University Press, 1995): 22. Qualifying this protest as a *drive* protest derives from my engagement with the notion of a "drive unconscious" as proposed by the Brazilian theorist and psychoanalyst João Perci Schiavon. See note 14.

40 This actually happened to Doce River (Rio Doce), Brazil, in Krenak's village, which is located on the left bank of that river in the municipality of Resplendor. At some point after the apparent death of the river (brought about by the devastating abuse of the Vale mining company), the river was found to be flowing

Notes to pp. 80–97

abundantly again, underground. See Ailton Krenak, "Em busca de uma terra sem tantos males," in *O lugar onde a terra descansa* (Rio de Janeiro: Núcleo de Cultura Indígena, 2000).

41 The word "banzo" comes from the *quimbundo* idiom of northeast of Angola. Aside from being a recurrent cause for suicide, this feeling, frequent among slaves, was also what gave rise to individual and collective escapes.

42 Translator's note: The same might be said about Donald Trump in the United States. When this book was published in Brazil, in the middle of 2018, Jair Bolsonaro was a federal deputy. He was elected president at the end of the same year.

43 See note 13 above.

44 "Resonance" differs from "empathy," another worn, overused word in our culture, now used in a way that's limited to a sense of shared opinions, ideologies, value systems, and feelings (psychological emotions), or, more precisely, "good feelings." In short, what "empathy" has come to denote is a sense of sharing limited to the sphere of the subject. Beyond the reduction of the term "empathy" to the macropolitical sphere and to the notion of "good feelings," what further negates the tensions proper to a relationship with alterity is the term's insertion into a lexicon of politically correct attitudes, attitudes which do not demand any kind of effective action or transformation of the "empathic" self on the basis of the real effects (the vital emotions) of the other on that self. In sum, the term "empathy" has been reduced to attitudes that disregard the micropolitical sphere, hence its inadequacy as a marker of that which makes cooperation viable in that sphere.

45 The expropriation of the drive always entails the expropriation of the movement that creates forms, given that this movement constitutes the essence of the drive. When expropriated and derailed from its ethical destiny (the production of new forms in the service of life), this movement loses its creating nature and becomes mere productivity: the production of forms in the service of the accumulation of capital.

46 On the idea of a "force of transindividual transformation," see Brian Massumi, *What Animals Teach Us about Politics* (Durham, NC: Duke University Press, 2014).

47 In 2018, when I wrote this essay, the threat of this kind of micropolitical violence was already felt in the air, and this, of course, is what led me to write about it. Nonetheless, at the time it was unthinkable that this threat would be fulfilled so quickly and so virulently, the way it has only four years later.

48 The financialization of the real-estate sector in Brazil is an example of the hegemony of globalized circuits of capital and finance in

164 Note to p. 98

the country through the opening of capital of local companies with shares on the stock exchanges. As Raquel Rolnik writes, at the end of the 1990s, significant changes begin to take place in the residential incorporation sector, with mergers, takeovers, and the arrival of equity funds and asset management companies. See Raquel Rolnik, *Urban Warfare Housing under the Empire of Finance* (New York: Verso, 2019), p. 212.

49 The plot of this new modality of the coup was conceived in a series of three meetings between right-wing politicians and center-right politicians from all over Latin America, with the participation of politicians from the United States. The purpose of the meetings was to establish an alliance and create a common plan based on shared ideas and strategies that could be adopted by these countries as they faced the rise of left-leaning governments. The first two meetings took place in Asunción, Paraguay, in 2010, and in Brasília in 2011. The decisive meeting took place in November 2012 in Atlanta. Twelve ex-presidents took part in this meeting, all of them right-wing or center-right politicians. Other leaders from the worlds of politics, economics, media, and the judicial branches were also in attendance. At the end of this meeting, the "Declaration of Atlanta" was released. The first summit of the Latin American Presidential Mission (Missão Presidencial Latino-Americana, MPL) was also instituted. Its purpose is manifest in two of the pronouncements made during the meetings: since we can't beat these communists in the voting booth, we will interrupt their administrations, protected by a veil of legality. These interruptions were referred to as "soft coups." The plural here and the way they are described already signal that this modality of the coup consists in a sequence of operations that take place successively and without explicit violence. The pretension of legality here is grounded on the manipulative narratives that this essay describes. In each one of these countries, the right wing had already begun to draw strategies, after the end of dictatorships, to impede the rise to power of left-leaning governments. This is what happened in Brazil, where soon after the return to democracy in 1985, and two decades before the meetings here summarized took place, generals from the armed forces concluded that, after the defeat of the guerrillas, the strategy of the left in its rise to power moved to the sphere of culture and to the area of institution building. Faced with this, the generals concluded, left-leaning governments should be repelled with the same weapons they themselves use, weapons that differed considerably from the weapons involved in Operation Condor (formally established in 1975, though functioning since the 1960s). Operation Condor was conceived by military governments in Latin America with the

Notes to pp. 98–103

collaboration of the United States. It emerged as a response to the armed struggles organized by the left as a way to fight military governments throughout the continent. From 1985 to 1988, these generals conceived a secret project called "Orvil." The title of this strategy is a muddling of the letters that make up the word "livro", "book", in Portuguese. This strategy differed from the one adopted by Operation Condor. The new strategy is conceived by means of books (and, now, by texts and images disseminated through social media), in contrast to the "condor strategy," based on the image of a bird that feeds on cadavers. In Portuguese, the term "condor" brings to mind the words *com dor*, "with pain"; inevitably, the actions taken under Operation Condor in Brazil are read as operations executed "with pain" or with the force of pain. It this sense, to call the new strategy of power, conceived in Atlanta, a "soft coup" is another way of saying that these are "painless" (or apparently painless) coups, in contrast to traditional coups, suffused with pain (*com dor*) as they are. Parts of this project were published internally by the Centro do Informações do Exército, Brazil's army information center, between 1989 and 1991. See João Cezar Castro Rocha, *Guerra cultural e retórica do ódio: crônicas de um Brasil pós-político* (Rio de Janeiro: Editora Caminhos, 2021).

50 Fernando Lugo was elected to the presidency in 2008 with the support of the Patriotic Alliance for Change, a coalition composed of more than a dozen social movements and opposition parties. His election brought an end to more than sixty-one years of presidential rule by the conservative, nationalist Colorado Party, founded in 1887 and controlled by Alfredo Stroessner during his years as dictator (1954–89). Lugo was impeached in 2012, in a process seen as a coup d'état by state leaders of the region. After Lugo's impeachment, his party won two more consecutive elections, in 2013 and again in 2018, when Mario Abdo Benítez, Stroessner's private secretary and the current president of Paraguay, was elected. Despite the fact that both elections were mired by scandal and fraud, and despite international outcry regarding the illegitimacy of both presidents elected after the coup, neither of these elections was nullified.

51 "Operação Lava-Jato," the name given to this operation, brings to mind an image of something cleaned thoroughly, with the force of water jets, the way cars are cleaned. The name of the operation, then, brings about images of a nation being washed clean of any corruption that soils it.

52 Dilma Vana Rousseff, a member of the Workers' Party in Brazil, was elected to the presidency after two successive presidential terms led by Lula. She held office from 2011 until her removal in 2016, following a process of impeachment.

Notes to pp. 104–114

53 Proposta de Emenda à Constituição (PEC), popularly known in Brazil as the "PEC to end the world," in reference to the high level of intended destruction at the heart of this proposed amendment.

54 An example of this is GP Investimentos, the first private equity firm to be listed on a stock market in Latin America. As Raquel Rolnik writes, it was founded in 1993 by Jorge Lemann and his partners at an investment bank, Banco Garantia, sold to Credit Suisse in 1998. GP Investimentos, Rolnik continues, either managed or outright controlled over fifty real-estate, infrastructure, retail, logistics, and telecommunications companies in Latin America. The firm is now based in the United States, Bermuda, Switzerland, and São Paulo. See Rolnik, *Urban Warfare Housing under the Empire of Finance*, p. 291.

55 Raquel Rolnik notes that CEOs from these investment firms ended up assuming executive positions in the construction companies their firms took over, thus collapsing administrative councils with management roles. See ibid., p. 292.

56 Brazil has one of the largest numbers of social media users in the world.

57 In some countries in Latin America, it is still possible to deploy the ghost of communism to cast a spell on the masses by linking communism to progressive leaders, especially during elections.

58 Félix Guattari suggests we understand "minority" in the singular sense, in contrast to what might be said to be the "majority" in the sense of being homogenous, proper to the hegemonic modes of existence of the dominant micropolitics under the capitalist regime. See Guattari and Rolnik, *Molecular Revolution in Brazil*. Deleuze also takes up this idea and discusses it in a text published in Brazil. See Deleuze, *Sobre o teatro: um manifesto de menos* (São Paulo: Ed. 34, 2010), pp. 59, 63–4.

59 This demonization still happens today. Recall, for instance, the way in which Judith Butler was linked to the figure of the witch in the attack mounted against her during her visit to Brazil in November 2017. Butler was in the country for a symposium entitled "The Ends of Democracy" ("Os fins da democracia"), which the philosopher co-organized. The demonizing portrayal of Butler was such that she was burned in effigy in front of the building where the symposium was taking place, the SESC Pompeia, one of the most respected cultural institutions in Brazil. Silvia Federici has written extensively on the category of the witch as a tool for the repression of women. See Federici, *Caliban and the Witch: Women, the Body and Primitive Accumulation* (Brooklyn, NY: Autonomedia, 2004). Translator's note: a novel recently published by Fernanda Melchor

Notes to pp. 115–116

is based on a murder that took place recently in Mexico. At the center of this real-life event and of the novelized account written by Melchor in her *Hurricane Season* is another gendered and sexually divergent figure demonized as a witch in order to justify violence against them. See Melchor, *Hurricane Season* (New York: New Directions, 2020).

60 The rate is contingent upon specific national histories of slave trading and genocidal extermination.

61 "Candomblé" (the word stands for "house for dances with tall hand drums") is an Afro-Brazilian religion. It emerged between the seventeenth and eighteenth centuries, deriving from African cults and their countless reinventions by the African diaspora. Its rituals revolve around the worship of natural forces, personified in the form of divine ancestors, the Orixás. Each human being is the child of different Orixás, with one Orixá being the main divine ancestor. Different Orixás and their respective configurations define the vital singularity of the vital potency of each human being. They are the forces that guide the exercise of this potency, an exercise that gets progressively refined through a process of initiation that lasts a lifetime. Candomblé persists to this day, despite the fact of its persecution dating back to the early years of slavery in Brazil. It began with the repression of religions that preceded Candomblé and it has returned cyclically and violently throughout the course of Brazilian history. Its persistence in the face of this persecution is evidence of the cultural resistance of both enslaved people from Africa and Afro-descendant Brazilians. There are several types of Candomblé, with different cosmogonies and different ritual practices. There are also several other Afro-American religions that share an origin with Candomblé and that also serve the cause of resistance: Cuban santería, Haitian voodoo, and Jamaican Obeah and Kumina, among others.

62 Black resistance has taken place in different ways and at different moments over the course of the history of slavery in Brazil. Black movements have achieved fundamental results in the last few decades alone. In the realm of state relations, during his first year in office, President Fernando Henrique Cardoso created an inter-agency working group charged with identifying actions and policies that made visible and deemed valuable the Black population in Brazil. This resulted in the creation of the Office of the Secretary for the Promotion of Racial Equality (Secretaria de Políticas de Promoção da Igualdade Racial, Seppir). These advances were further promoted during the government of President Lula, with the enactment of government programs and legislative measures such as the 2012 Lei de Cotas, which cemented into law minimum college

168 Notes to pp. 119–130

admission quotas for Black, mixed-raced, indigenous, *quilombola*, poor, and other underrepresented applicants. In recent years, as attacks on it have grown more vicious, the Black movement in Brazil has been expanding and gaining in strength in the micropolitical sphere. Theirs has turned into a ceaseless intervention into racialized dynamics, which has resulted in effective exposure of the embedded presence of racism acrosss social sectors. It's worth remembering that slavery inscribed and naturalized racism in the subjectivity of Brazilians, and that racism so inscribed has remained a constant throughout the country's history.

63 Michel Miguel Elias Temer Lulia was the thirty-seventh president of Brazil, from August 31, 2016, to January 1, 2019. He was the vice-president during Dilma Rousseff's presidency and actively colluded in her impeachment.

64 Pará and Amapá are two of the twenty-seven states that form the Federative Republic of Brazil. Both states are located in the north of the country, bordering Suriname and French Guiana. A large proportion of their territory is made up of the Amazon forest.

65 Renca stipulated that only the Companhia de Pesquisa de Recursos Minerais (CPRM), a public company held by the Mining and Energy Ministry (Ministério de Minas e Energia), could perform research in order to assess mining activity in the reserve. In 2022, the savage exploitation (with support from the state) of this and other Amazonian lands (lands inhabited by indigenous peoples) reached lethal levels.

66 Presidential decrees in Brazil, like executive orders in the United States, do not require congressional approval.

67 The improvements in the quality of life of the most disenfranchised segments of Brazilian society during the administrations of Lula and Dilma are remarkable: 57 million people make up these segments of society, which constitutes 30 percent of the population living at or below the poverty line, with a family income of R$387.07 per day or less. During Lula's presidency, between 2001 and 2008, the proportion of people in Brazil living at or below the poverty line fell from 30 to 15 percent (from 57 million to fewer than 30 million people). Between 2001 and 2015, the poorest in Brazil saw an increase of their income equivalent to 11 to 12 percent.

68 This essay was written in 2018, when Trump was still president of the United States and when Bolsonaro's presidential campaign was just getting started. Bolsonaro was elected in October 2018.

69 São Bernardo do Campo is one of three locations of the metal-working industry in Brazil, together with Santo André and São Caetano do Sul. The three sites, collectively, are known as the ABC Paulista. During the years of the dictatorship, the headquarters of

Notes to pp. 130–144

the São Bernardo do Campo Metalworkers' Union was the locus of civil unrest calling for the redemocratization of Brazil. The unrest became known as the "Diretas já" movement. During these years, Lula was a two-term president of the union and, because of his work, was persecuted, indicted, and imprisoned in 1980. This was the year in which he served as founding leader of the Workers' Party, and this was the beginning of his political career. He ran for governor in São Paulo state in 1982 but lost. His first electoral victory came in 1986, when he was elected to represent the state in the National Congress. Soon after that, and while he was in the National Congress, the new constitution was drafted. Later, Lula ran three times for president and lost all three times. He won on his fourth attempt, in 2002, and was reelected in 2006.

70 In order to understand what kind of figure Maroni is, it is enough to recall that he was convicted and imprisoned several times, beginning in 2007, on charges of organizing prostitution in his "nightclubs" and doing so without the permits and certificates required by law. More recently, in 2021, during the Covid-19 pandemic, his nightclub was closed after it failed to implement the required measures to prevent the spread of the virus. Against government regulations, Maroni kept his club open for business, packed to the brim with customers who did not wear masks or practice social distancing. That same year, Maroni was freed on bail and his nightclub reopened.

71 In 2021, when the STF halted proceedings and quashed convictions against Lula, Antunes Rocha, still a judge but no longer president of the STF, changed her opinion and voted in favor of Lula's acquittal.

72 The term "gang of criminals" (*quadrillha de criminosos, quadrilhão do PT*) was used to describe members of the Workers' Party in the narrative employed in the coup series. This language was widely disseminated and became inscribed in the memory of most Brazilians, many of whom still take it to be true when used in reference to members of the Workers' Party.

73 Eduardo Cunha is an example of this. He presided over Congress when Dilma Rousseff was impeached. Once that work was completed, in September of that same year, he was accused of corruption and money laundering and deposed. He is unable to run for office until 2026. He was also imprisoned.

74 The *Centrão* is an informal block made up of legislators linked to center and right-wing parties. Most of them have been accused of corruption. They come together to guarantee for themselves illegal advantages and favors in exchange for their approval of measures proposed by the executive. The name *Centrão* harks back to the

170   Notes to pp. 145–147

majoritarian block that came together as part of the Constitutive Assembly of 1988.

75 Geraldo Alckmin was city councillor and mayor in Pindamonhangaba, the city where he was born, in the interior of São Paulo state. He was state and federal legislator and a two-term governor of São Paulo and ran for the presidency on several occasions, losing every time. Until recently, he was a member of a center/center-right party, the Partido da Social Democracia Brasileira (PSDB), which he co-founded (the party mixes together social-democratic, Christian democratic, and social and economic liberal leanings). This party was founded in 1988, after the end of the dictatorship. It steadfastly opposed the administrations of the Workers' Party. In 2021, Alckmin joined the Partido Socialista Brasileiro (PSB).

76 Consider, for instance, the *movimento integralista*, an earlier fascist outbreak that emerged in Brazil in the 1930s. It was a notably large movement that managed to gather the support of about 1,300,000 Brazilians by 1938. That year, the movement was declared illegal by the Estado Novo. The number of people who subscribed to this movement is small compared to the masses of people who identify with Bolsonaro's government. Plínio Salgado, one of the leaders of the *integralista* movement, ran for the presidency and managed to receive only 7 percent of the votes. This figure is dwarfed by the 49 percent of votes Bolsonaro received in his last bid for the presidency. It is worth noting that there are movements active at present which see themselves carrying the legacy of the *integralista* movement. Among these are Ação Integralista Revolucionária (AIR[40]), the Movimento Integralista e Linearista Brasileiro (MIL-B) and the Frente Integralista Brasileira (FIB).

CRITICAL SOUTH

"In this book, Suely Rolnik dismantles the stable partitions between the micropolitical and the macropolitical. She maps out how to understand their internal vectors (reactionary and emancipatory) rather than reinforcing their simple binarism. Moreover, here shines a precise and precious definition of the colonial as that which makes us distrust the knowledge of the body. For that, this book is also proposed as a practical manual, part of a collective task, which makes the decolonization of the unconscious an anti-fascist practice."

VERÓNICA GAGO, feminist activist and professor at the University of Buenos Aires

As the globalized regime of neoliberal capitalism consolidates its grip on the world, it refines the micropolitics proper to the capitalist system and makes it more perverse. This micropolitics involves the appropriation – what Suely Rolnik calls the "pimping" – of life, as it turns the life drive itself away from creation and cooperation and towards the deadening, destructive practice necessary for capital accumulation. This dynamic is the engine of what Rolnik calls the colonial-capitalistic unconscious regime. She also identifies the conditions necessary to fight against this regime – namely, a reappropriation of the life drive, the energetic basis at the heart of all life forms, human life included, and the principal source of extraction for capitalism.

Drawing on examples from across the Americas, including Brazil and the United States, Rolnik examines the circumstances that have given rise to regressive, reactionary governments throughout the world. These circumstances include, at the macro level, an alliance between neoliberalism and extreme conservatism and, at the micro level, a crisis of the hegemonic subject in the face of the emergent empowerment of marginalized communities that practice other modes of subjectivation.

This crucial book by one of the most prominent intellectuals in Latin America today will be of great value to anyone interested in contemporary politics and social struggles.

SUELY ROLNIK is a psychoanalyst and Professor of Clinical Psychology at the Pontifical Catholic University of São Paulo.

Cover image Gioconda Kunhã © Denilson Baniwa
Cover design Sunandini Banerjee, Seagull Books

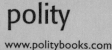
www.politybooks.com